FINANCIAL MANAGEMENT

By the Same Author

- Financial Services in India
- Portfolio Management (Including Security Analysis)
- Financial Markets and Institutions
- Research Methodology in Social Sciences
- Management of Financial Institutions in India
- Management of Financial Markets and Services in India (In Press)

About the Author

Dr. G. Ramesh Babu obtained his degree of Ph.D in Industrial Finance. With his vast teaching experience of 23 years at UG and PG levels, he is presently serving Department of Commerce, SSRJ College, Khammam.

He also conducts classes for Treasury and Income Tax Departments besides several other courses. He has contribution of publishing many papers in journals of repute, holding membership of professional bodies, and papers accepted at International and national seminars.

Financial Management

G. Ramesh Babu

CONCEPT PUBLISHING COMPANY PVT. LTD.
NEW DELHI-110 059

ISBN-13: 978-81-8069-754-8 (HB)
ISBN-13: 978-81-8069-755-5 (PB)

First Published 2012

Published and Printed by

Concept Publishing Company Pvt. Ltd.
Regd. Office:
A/15-16, Commercial Block, Mohan Garden
New Delhi-110059 (India)
Phones : 25351460, 25351794, *Fax* : 091-11-25357109
Email : publishing@conceptpub.com
Website: www.conceptpub.com

Editorial Office:
H-13, Bali Nagar, New Delhi-110 015, India.

Cataloging in Publication Data--*Courtesy:* D.K. Agencies (P) Ltd. <docinfo@dkagencies.com>

Ramesh Babu, G. (Gunda), 1963-
Financial management / G. Ramesh Babu.
p. cm.
Includes index.
ISBN 9788180697548

1. Business enterprises--India--Finance. 2. Capital budget--India--Case studies. I. Title.

DDC 338.70954 22

Preface

The new economic policy aims at rapid and substantial economic growth and integration with the global economy in a harmonized manner. It transformed successively towards a market oriented economy. The globe is rotating on the flow of money. After reforms, the financial sector has grown tremendously. Modern economics is highly influenced by expansion and diversification. Globalisation has changed the world business environment. The creation of wealth by a nation could be done through powerful weapons such as "capital, technology, human resources". These weapons can be applied to counter the poverty.

Finance is provision of money. In this book an attempt is made to give a comprehensive coverage of Financial Management. Since the book is synthesis. I thank all authors who have contributed to the world of finance. I have made acknowledgments of every idea whose sources have been identified. It is my response to thank Smt. K. Meenakshi, President, Jyothi Education Society, Smt. Indira Parimi, Vice Chairman, Jyothi Education Society, Hyderabad. I am thankful to Sri K. Harihara Prasad, Principal, S.S.R.J. College, Khammam I wholeheartedly thank Prof. P. Madhusudan Rao, Prof. V. Gangadhar, Prof. Rajeshan of the Department of Commerce and Business Management, Kakatiya University, Warangal, Prof. Om Prakash, Head, Department of Commerce, Prof. B. Venkata Rathnam, Chairman, Board of Studies, Kakatiya University.

I would like to express my warm and cordial thanks to my well wishers, Prof. Jilani, University of Hyderabad, Prof. Raubrahman, University of Hyderabad, Prof. Chordia, Suryadatta Institute of Management, Pune, Prof. Harikrishna Maran, Bangalore, Mr. Sadasivapuri, Chartered Accountant, Srinagar, Dr. Jayanthi, Imphal, Mrs. Elizebath Shillong, for their spontaneous help in so many ways in my endevour. I am specially thankful to Smt. P. Sailaja for improving the manuscript.

I owe my gratitude to Shri Ashok Kumar Mittal, Shri Nitin Kumar Mittal and Sri S.P. Sinha of Concept Publishing Company Pvt. Ltd. for giving their personal attention in expediting the process of this book.

Dr. G. Ramesh Babu,
E mail: gunda_rameshbabu@yahoo.co.in.

Contents

1

Introduction

The management of a business concern is a complex activity. The functional areas of management can deal more specifically is related to their specialized areas. A Financial Management is one of the specified area line management. It is related to supply the funds to the corporate sector. It deals with the efficient utilization of financial resources. Finance is the important aspect in handling business aspects. Finance is provision of money. Financial management reveals the better utilization of money. Any mismanagement of finance causes a lot of trouble to the corporate sector. Efficient utilization of funds is one of the important factors in determination of success in commercial entities.

Finance involves rising of funds and creates a good environment for better functioning of the corporate sector without interruption of business activities. The management of a company should utilize financial management as a weapon to achieve their desired goal. A human being with the provision of money carries out all activities on the earth. Money can do all the affairs of the routine activities of a commercial enterprise. A timely payment of all expenses made by a commercial enterprise enhances the good reputation of the concern. A company through different ways can earn goodwill. It provides the way to reach higher satisfaction levels of the customers, shareholders, employees, investors and suppliers. Management is a combination of the different functional areas. Each aspect stimulates the higher levels of the productivity of the business concern. All the functional areas of management such as marketing, production, human relations, research, and development have a lot to do with finance function.

Finance plays a useful and constructive role in discharge of various policy decisions to be taken by top-level management of the corporate sector. It occupies in strategy formulation planning, decision-making and policy control activities of the corporate sector. In the digital era, finance is the foundation of all kinds of economic activities. The kingpin element provides access to all sources. It is true that money generates money. Money always chases money. Money is always haunted by money. Financial management is the agricultural science of the money. It deals with the cultivation of the money. It always reflects the better yield of crop, which is based on soil fertility. Financial management is like heart of a human being. Heart is the important and restless organ of the body. If the failure of heart organ, no survival of the human being on the earth. Heart functions from the birth to death of the human being.

Financial Management can be compared with the heart ORGAN. It work restless and pumps blood in a properly manner to recalculate in the body. Finance also circulates in the organization. The velocity of money depends upon managerial capacity of the top-level management. Any business organization on the earth works for profit. Profit is the main important ingredient in abets delicacies cuisine. It is inner element in all business organizations respiration. Capital is oxygen profit is carbon dioxide of the respiration. A plenty of available oxygen made respiration more easily and with high velocity. Profit is a hungry element for the business concern. Any amount of profit earned by the corporate enterprise should reach to the satisfactory levels of shareholders. Shareholders satisfaction is the most crucial element in the management of a business concern. The shareholders also see the welfare of the employs. In India, management of human being is biggest task before any kind of commercial enterprise. Machines, material can be controlled but men could not control. Selling price is a combination of various kinds of expenses such as production, office, finance, selling and distribution. In the modern world, every organization is concentrating on reduction of selling price due to heavy competition in the market. All companies introduced cost reduction programmers in their functional areas of management. At present market consists with full of competition. Competition is a good phenomenon to the consumer. The competition can increase the managerial and technical expertism of the industry. Innovation, creativity and new technological process will be exploited and captured by the industrial organizations. Hence, all the hidden talent will became asset to the human being. The Competition stimulates the higher levels of the productivity of the corporate sector. In the tough competition, only expertise, talent, skilled committed organizations can survive. The creation of the competition is possible only with the introduction of the reforms. Reforms are also useful to the corporate sector to grow beyond the levels of expatriation. Reforms in the economic aspects have been changed India completely towards a new destination. It may not be surprise, the life style of a non-professional in the United States and India may become equal in near future. India is a huge market for best–planned strategic companies. The policy-makers should be think about the stimulations of the buying capacity of the rural people. The entire India is located in rural areas. The Government should develop agricultural sector to boost up the purchasing capacity of the rural fellows. The new technology should be invented to utilize the natural resources from rural areas. Village infrastructure is the key element in the development of a nation. A high-level dose of liberalization can create wondes in the economy. A strong committed administration can influence the standard of living of the people in the country. The policy-makers should be remember that, wealth creation is only a way to become prosperous in the digital era.

Meaning of Financial Management: Business needs money to make more money. A money will grow, if it properly managed. The management capabilities will be reflected in the efficient management resources. Financial resources are one of the significant factors to achieve the desired goal of a firm. The term business finance may be defined, "as the provision of money at the it is wanted." Finance may be defined, "as procurement of funds and their effective utilization." Financial management is concerned with these aspects. The efficiency of a corporate enterprise can be measured through financial, technical, and marketing capabilities. Even the kinds know the money and its uniqueness, importance and prescience. There is no excuse if our well-trained managers do not focus their attention on important aspect of existence, survival, and growth. Financial management is a dynamic subject. It deals with all aspects of functional management. The basic aim of any enterprise is to earn profit from market opportunities. Profit conscious makes the company to become a blue-chip organization. It deals with past, present and future. The management makes use of various financial techniques devices for administrat the financial affairs of the firm. Financial management monitors the better effective utilization of financial resources in order to achieve the firm's desired goal. It observes about profits or losses of the firm. It closely observes regarding mismatch of asset liabilities of the firm. It deals with past, present and future abilities of the firm. It occupies an important role in formulation of strategic plans. A proper financial planning makes the vision and dreams are translated into the reality. Professional managers with a thorough understanding of the finance get a sense of the proper direction to achieve the goal. Management of finance is both an art and science. Indian home-maker is the best expert in finance to handle domestic affairs with a little amount of husband's earnings. The finance managers should learn many things from them. Hence, financial management is related with the proper management of funds.

The 'Financial Managements is concerned with the efficient use of an important economic resources namely capital funds.'– Solomon.

'Business finance can broadly be defined, "as the activity concerned with planning, raising, controlling and administering of the funds used in the business."–Gateman and Dougall, corporate financial policy p.1.

Objectives of Financial Management: Financial management is closely related with better utilization of financial resources. It has two objectives. 1. basic objectives, 2. Ancillary objectives.

Traditionally, as the basic objectives of the financial management are associated with maintenance of liquid assets and maximization of profitability of the commercial enterprise. Liquidity is an important element in the corporate sector. Liquidity means, the business enterprise should be able to pay its obligations at all times. Maintenance of liquid assets is not an easy task. A well and proper planned financial strategy would make the firm to keep always at liquid position. This situation will boost up goodwill of the company. A prompt payment of outstanding due amount, without any post payment makes the business as enterprise to cultivate for further business transactions with more velocity. The speed of business transactions enhances the efficiency levels of the business enterprise. The velocity of business transactions can create confidence among the suppliers and market forces. *Profit Maximisation* is anther important and inner element of the commercial enterprise. The *Profit* is oxygen to the commercial enterprise. Profit consciousness is the heart beating of the enterprise. A business enterprise will survive unto earning profitability; otherwise, it will be wound up. Profit earning depends upon many factors. It cannot be predicted. It is based on market. It depends upon the efficiency of the business enterprise. In some situations, adequate financial resources may not generate reasonable profits. The business is involved in risk and uncertainty. Risk is an estimated future loss of a business concern. Risk and return is the game of market. Risk always chases return. The intelligent businessperson should escape risk and capture return. Goodwill of the firm will stimulate the higher levels of profitability. Goodwill will be earned by a business concern through different manners. Liquidity helps to maintain and retain goodwill of the concern in the market. Goodwill is an intangible asset, which creates loyalty to the customers. In a highly competitive environment, their role occupies a significant factor to survive in the market. A Customers desire; needs, convenient cannot be ignored by the corporate sector. Customer loyalty is an important and significant factor to swim in the market.

The financial management is one of the concerned managerial decision, which result in acquiring, and financing of long and short-term credits for the firm. It deals with the selection of specified financial instrument or a combination of liabilities, as well as the problem of size and growth of a business enterprise.

A business firm is a profit conscious organization. Profit is an inner desire of any commercial enterprise. Profit maximization has come under severe criticism because of several reasons.

1. Profit maximization does not quantify the earnings how much of profit to be earned. What rate of profit to be captured from the market.
2. Profit maximization does not help in making a decision projects giving different benefits over a period.
3. Profit maximization does not help in social responsibility of the business. Businessperson always giving priority to earn profit rather than welfare of the customer and society. Too much of profit earning may leads to exploitation of the customers. Generally, business enterprise needs stability in the market. Stability will be acquired through strong sales. Some firms are willing to

accept lower profits with high volume of sales. Profit maximi- zation does not take into consideration of welfare. Now a days it is not considered an ideal criteria for making investment and financing decisions. *Prof. Ezrasolman* has recommended wealth maximization as best criteria for making decisions. Wealth maximization is considered the main objective of the financial management. It is related to maximizing the economic welfare of the shareholders of a company. Wealth maximization can be defined as *'The Gross Present Worth of a Course of Action is equal to the Capitalised Value of the flow of Future Expected Benefits, discounted at the rate which reflects their certainity or Uncertainity,* Prof. Ezrasoloman

Wealth Occupies a significant role in the prosperity. Prosperity of a nation is strongly built up with wealth resources. Wealth is the difference between gross present worth and the investment required to achieve the goal. As per the theory any financial action can be taken if the net present worth above zero. Business provides number of alternatives, and then the decision should be taken which creates most wealth or greatest amount of net present worth. The value of company will be stimulated by its net worth. The net worth of a company is highly influenced by many factors. The value of a company share depends upon largely on earning capacity. The earning capability will be reflected through sales. Customers generate sales. A strong and large customer's base will stimulate the earning per share. Earning per share is an important barometer to measure the efficiency of the commercial enterprise. Therefore, a financial manager should follow a policy to reflect profitability in every financial action decision.

Ancillary Objectives plays an important role in financial management. The other objectives of the financial management are one. A reasonable return to shareholders. 2. stimulation of technical, managerial and financial efficiency. 3. financial discipline.

Return is a reward to the shareholders. Shareholders are the owners of the business enterprise. They provide money to generate more money. Money creates money. The financial manager of the company should always take a financial action, which enhances the profitability levels of the industrial houses. Shareholders should be rewarded with reasonable dividend or capital appreciation. The company will pay dividend to the shareholders. Shareholders will satisfy with the performance of the company through dividend or bonus issue. The demographic analysis of the shareholders will decide quantum amount of dividend. In this juncture, the financial manager of the company should behave like a trustee of the shareholders.

The Operational Efficiency is another important factor in the evaluation of a commercial enterprise. Efficiency reflects abilities. Abilities are different combination of specified activities. Usually all enterprises shall have manufacturing, marketing, financial abilities in order to reach the goal of a firm. Manufacturing abilities can be learned through adoption of latest technology. Technology is an important element in the digital era. It reduces cost of production and save time. A higher level of probable profit awaits the shareholders due to adoption of scientific technology. Technology occupies a dominant role in the development of a nation. A strong technological development makes the nation as a knowledge management force. Knowledge is a barometer for efficiency. It reflects the skills and expertise. Technical abilities will definitely helps the company to deliver the goods utmost quality products. Quality is unforgettable element in the market. Customer always desire higher quality products at lower prices. Marketing abilities can boost the higher level of the profitability. A high quality of products will be sold in the market easily with the best marketing forces at affordable price. Marketing expertise always searching for a better sale price to enhance the profitability. It provides price opportunity, discovers new markets, new customers and reflects in the achievement of goal. Financial abilities can afford the company to smooth functioning of all business activities without any interruption in production. A smooth flow of all activities and transactions can leads to build up stability in the market. A stability position in the market makes the company to build a strong reserves and surplus in the company. A company with fat results can go for expansion or diversification. The situation nourishes development of the corporate sector. The financial management provides a safety cushion to the top-level management for carrying out the developmental process of the enterprise. It can help to raise large amount of resources from the market. It always searching for low cost funds. It monitors the efficient utilization of financial resources.

Financial discipline is most important factor to achieve the desired goal of the firm. Discipline is a significant factor to earn goodwill. Goodwill creates wealth. Wealth is a reflection of prosperity of a company. It stimulates the higher level of the profitability. It is involved with various rules and regulations. Rules are framed for better functioning of the system.

Scope of Financial Management: Financial management is a subject of growing interest at present. It became as an academic discipline. It was separated from economics branch. The role of financial manager has undergone several changes recently. It is a dynamic subject. It always works for achieving desired goal of the firm. The scope of financial management can be studied as follows:

The Traditional approach was popular in past. It has a limited role in raising and administrating of funds by the corporate sector. The financial manager of the corporate sector was restricted to the limited role in the management. He was a person to look after the financial needs of the business enterprise. He had been instrumental force in arrangement of funds from market through a proper financial instrument. He had also taken a part to take a legal accounting relationship between the company and lenders. According to traditional approach, the finance manager has to keep accurate financial records, prepare corporate reports and making payments in time. The traditional approach was evolved in 1920. The term corporate finance was used in place of the present term financial management. Thomas Greek wrote the corporate finance. It was given further impetus by Edward Meade in 1910. In 1919, another book *the Financial Policy of Corporation* was brought by Arthur Dewing. It dominated the academic world in the field of corporate finance. For three decades, the traditional approach was dominated up to 1950. After that period, it had severely criticized and abandoned due to various reasons. Traditional approach has been failed due to the following reasons:

(a) It ignored financial problems of the commercial enterprise. It gives importance during the course of incorporation, mergers, acquisition, consolidation, and reorganization only. It failed to solve the routine financial problems of the company.

(b) It had failed to take internal financial decisions. This method was restricted with raising and administering of funds. It completely observes financial affairs from the view of suppliers of funds.

(c) It does not take into consideration of the problems of non-corporate industrial houses.

(d) It concentrated only on long-term finance of the corporate sector. However, short-term finance needs also to be given top priority. It completely ignored the working capital management element in the corporate finance. Working capital occupies a dominant role in smooth functioning of a business entity.

Modern approach has emerged, as technological and widened marketing operations exist in the business environment. After 1950, the business environment changed and made it imperative to make optimum use of available resources for the corporate sector. The exposed information with the help of computers the financial manager could make sound decisions. Computers are powerful tools in application of various scientific analyses in operation research. Hence, the scope of financial management increased with the introduction of capital budgeting techniques. The modern approach developed various pricing models, valuation models, and investment portfolio theories. It is concerned with acquisition and allocation of funds. It views the term financial management in a broader sense. It is related to wide use of funds and to achieve the broad financial goals of the firm. It analysis in a new way to study the financial problems of a firm. This approach deals with volume of funds kind of asset sources of resources available. Therefore, the financial management scope has been presented below:

(a) Funds estimation.
(b) Provision of funds.
(c) Investment decision.
(d) Dividend decision.

Funds Estimation is an important function to be performed by finance manager. The finance manager of a modern corporate should make a careful observation about fund requirement. He should take into consideration of fixed and working capital requirements of the business enterprise. Proper careful forecasting the activities of business enterprises will do it. He should make a thorough analysis of all activities.

Provision of Funds is another important factor in determination of scope of financial management. The business enterprise should be provided with sufficient amount of financial resources to carry out the business activities very smoothly. The fund should be made available to the company at the proper time of requirement. The finance manager has the responsibility to ru0n the business enterprise without interruption in production activities. He has to identify the sources of finance at lowest possible cost of funds. He has to estimate the quantum of money to be raised and other consequences involved in that manner. He has to maintain a proper balance between fixed and non-fixed cost bearing securities. He has to evaluate various alternatives for better sources of finance. The finance manager should be well equipped with various capital structure theories in practice. He should know all consequences with effect of adoption of different alternatives.

Investment Decision is another important factor in financial management. It is related to investment of financial resources in both capital and current assets. The modern finance manager has to evaluate different investment proposals and select the best one for the welfare of the firm. Investment is a curb of present desires. Investment is a sacrifice element.

Dividend Decision is one of the important and inner elements for the financial manager of a business entity. Every financial manager think about to offer higher rate of dividend to the shareholders. He is the trustee for shareholder's money. A strong dividend policy is necessary for keeping shareholders happily. Dividend is a reward to the investor. A large amount of earnings will make the company to pay hefty dividends to the shareholders. However, the rate of dividend declaration is highly influenced by many factors. The top-level management decides the distribution of profits, which is a represent organ of shareholders. In practice, the dividend announcement is determined by market price of the share, earnings of the company, tax position of shareholders. Therefore, the retention of profit depends upon company's situation. The finance manager should keep in his mind about the ratio of distribution between retention and payout.

The four important factors indicate about the behaviour of the financial management in different aspects. Acquisition of funds and allocation is a highly intellectual factor in achieving the desired goal of a firm. Allocation and acquisition influence the firm's production, marketing, and other functions. They also affect the firm's size, growth, risk, and profitability. The modern financial manager should take proper decision in acquisition and allocation of funds. The traditional function has been limited to only acquisition of money. However, the modern approach broadened the role of finance manager in achieving the goal of the firm. He has to concern more about determining the size of the firm, and adoption of better technology in order to achieve higher productivity. He set the peace and growth of the company, prepares profit planning, and set the combination of asset mix in a commercial enterprise. The modern finance manager has to work with more cautiously. Apart from these four functions, he has to follow several factors in achieving the goal of the firm. The finance manager should ensure to supply of funds to all parts of the company. He should observe the financial performance of the organization and take proper decision at appropriate time. He has to negotiate with all officials of the financial institutions and found suppliers. Therefore, the financial management has emerged and helps to solve many problems in the corporate sector.

Liquidity and Profitability: The task of financial manager is changing in a highly competitive business environment. He has to look after several financial issues in order to achieve the firm's goal. Therefore, he should give priority for two important elements such as the liquidity and profitability. Liquidity means ability to pay cash for its commitment. If a company is able to meet its unexpected large purchases, it is said to be liquid company. Keeping sufficient resources of finance is known as liquidity. Every firm has cash reserves to meet contingencies at any time. Profitability means earning capacity of a firm. It reveals efficient use of funds to get more return. Liquidity and profitability are very closely related. If liquidity increases profitability decreases. The balance between these two factors determines the ability of the finance manager. If a firm concentrates on profitability, the firm is endangered in liquidity. There is a similar comparison between risk and return. Risk and return is the game of competitive market. Market is a combination of a desires and dreams. It is based on customer's needs and convenience. High-risk decisions yield high returns. The return of a company is highly influenced by several factors. The manager of the company should choose risk and return. He should be able to run the company in an optimum utilization of resources of the entity. He should take all steps to better utilization of men, machine and money resources. He has to extract all these resources to achieve the desired goal of the firm. He should be able to predict accurately. Business is a guesswork, which depends upon several elements. The business environment is providing different opportunities to the corporate sector. The corporate sector should choose the best alternative in order to capture the return. Return is generated from risk. Risk can be avoid and unavoidable in some situations. An efficient finance manager should avoid risk and attract return. The finance manager should be able to predict accurate cash inflows, which lead to liquidity. Liquidity boosts the reputation of the firm. Cost control and forecasting future sales leads to profitability. Managing flow of funds paves, the prediction of future inflows generates profits. Hence, business is based on cash inflows and outflows. Principled inflows and outflows may create good environment for the corporate sector. The welfare of the shareholders depends upon better utilization of resources that managed by a company with the help of the experts. However better expertise talent skill managerial experience capabilities market environment and other all factors will influence the level of profitability of the corporate sector. Therefore, every finance manager should see that the share price should be higher in stock market at appropriate times.

Methods and Tools of Financial Management: Finance is a provision of money at desired time. Acquisition and allocation of a money is the utmost careful function of modern finance manager. The finance manager has to take several decisions in discharge of his duties. He uses various methods and techniques to the goal of the firm. Procurement of funds can be made through various sources of finance. The finance manager as per the requirement of the company obtains funds from cheapest sources. The requirement of funds can be long and short-term. Long-term funds may be procured from shareholders, debenture holders, from financial institutions banks and investors. Short-term finance will be acquired from commercial banks, public deposits, and suppliers of goods. The financial manager should be able to design best capital structure of the firm, keeping in view of shareholders welfare. He must be keep in his mind about maximization of the shareholders wealth. He must be able to analyze in various situations about financial advantage in order to get the goals. He should also observe about evaluating different capital expenditure alternatives for the welfare of shareholders. He must be efficient in analysis of capital budgeting techniques. Capital budgeting requires a strong analytical abilities regarding average rate of return. Payback, internal rate of return, net present value, and profitability index. Capital budgeting is useful in accepting or rejecting a project. Financial management always observes the better utilization of resources. It measures effectiveness of a business enterprises actions and decisions. A firm can increase its profitability without affecting its liquidity. Maintenance of balance between liquidity and profitability is the barometer of its efficiency. A strong and efficient management of working capital would be reflected in its profitability. Following are the important financial tools:

(a) Cost of Capital.
(b) Leverage.
(c) Capital Budgeting.
(d) Funds Flow Analysis.
(e) Ratio Analysis.
(f) Cash Flow Analysis.

Cost of Capital is an important tool for the financial manager. It helps the manager to raise finance from cheap cost of funds. It is also helpful to determine optimum capital structure. The finance manager is the trustee of shareholders. Every decision of financial manager should provide the funds at the lowest cost of recurring expenses to the business enterprise. His aim must be profit maximization.

Advantage is another important tool to the modern corporate financial manager. Advantage is an explanation for different kinds of expenses incurred by the commercial enterprise. It is useful for comparison of various expenses among companies. The financial manager can take a decision with the help of cost control activities. The finance manager of a company can implement cost reduction programme in order to reduce the cost of production. If the company is able to the produce at low cost, then the company can earn higher profits. Hence, the profit maximization desire can be achieved through this tool.

Capital Budgeting is a highly specialized technical tool in financial management. Business is a chance of opportunity. It is always uncertainty. It provides both risk and return. In the business environment, risk is unwanted guest. No businessperson can invite it. Every businessperson thinks about return. Return is reward to the entrepreneur. Business provides several opportunities. The entrepreneur should evaluate all alternatives. The modern financial manager utilizes to the capital budgeting technique in the selection of a right project at right time. Capital budgeting is a technique, which explains all consequences in advance. Therefore, the financial manager could use better techniques to accept the good project otherwise, it may be misfired.

Funds Flow Analysis is another important tool in the financial management. The statement of funds flow analysis reveals the movement of funds for better utilization of the company. Funds flow statement is an important source for further analysis in financial management.

Ratio Analysis is a powerful technique in the financial management. It deals with the financial status of the company. It indicates the healthy position of a business enterprise. It is a litmus test to decide the efficiency of a person who involved in a business. Ratio analysis is a postmortem of business transactions. The success or failure of a business enterprise can be reviewed.

Cash Flow Analysis is one of the tools in financial management. It reveals the cash position of the company, it observes about the movement of cash flows. Cash is the important element in business transactions. The velocity of the business transactions depends upon the cash position. Cash is always a desirable liquid asset. It indicates the financial strength of a business entity.

Financial Management and Other Areas of Management: The success of a business enterprise depends upon its capabilities. Generally, every corporate entity should have technical, managerial, and financial capabilities. In the business, environment efficiency is an important tool to achieve the desired goal of the firm. The technical abilities lie with the adopted technology. *Technology* is the most important which highly influential factor in arriving cost of production. A low cost of product with high quality can generate more profit. The managerial capacity lies with the top-level management. The top-level management is a combination of different portfolios of experts. A pool of different expert's decision may not be wrong at all times. Their prediction will be based on logical explanation. Financial capabilities are another important area of management. Finance is a growing of importance. It explains about the better utilization of fund for productive purpose. Finance is like blood, which circulates entire the body. All activities of the organization can be carried out with the help of finance. Financial management is an applied field of business administration. There will be a close relationship between financial management and other areas of management. They are presented below:

(a) Financial Management and Financial Accounting
(b) Financial Management and Cost Accounting
(c) Financial Management and Asset Management
(d) Financial Management and Marketing Management
(e) Financial Management and Personnel Management

Financial management and financial accounting are quite different. Financial accounting is related to keep the record of already existed business transactions. It records summarizes all business transactions on day-to-day basis. Financial management is concerned about utilization of resources. It measures the efficiency of the business enterprises. Financial accounting is a tool for providing information to the finance manager. All financial affairs will be recorded, reported, and measured. This information is enabling to take a decision by the financial manager. It is a data collection process. Financial management is a managerial decision-making process. It is related to the management of funds. The basic objective of financial accounting is to keep all monetary affairs in a systematic way. The important statements are prepared by input sources of financial accounting. Profit and Loss Account, Balance Sheet is prepared for a certain period. Profit and Loss Account reflects the profit earned by a company. The net profit is available in this account after making several financial consequences of financial affairs. Balance Sheet exposes the financial position of the company as on a particular date. Financial management on the other hand is helpful to procure the funds at lowest possible cost. It also ensures that funds are available at the right time. Financial management and financial accounting is complementary to each other. These are concerned with the ascertainment of actual profits. The Profit and Loss Account reveals the actual profit earned by a company. The profit is the basis for computation of earning per share. EPS is the vital important factor in the financial management. Dividend is a reward to the investor. The finance manager with the help of information will declare the rate of dividend available from financial accounting department. The quantum of profit will be arrived by the financial accounting department. The rate of dividend will be determined by the dividend policy of the company. Dividend policy is the part of financial management. Capital budgeting is an important technique in the financial management. The inputs are supplied by the financial accounting. Therefore, financial management is concerned with the decision-making, while financial accounting is providing all information. Working capital management is an important factor in financial management. The inputs for preparation of working capital management are cash budget. The cash budget will be prepared by the information available from financial accounting department. A careful preparation of working capital management stimulates the reputation in higher levels. However, financial accounting and financial management are quite different but they are useful in decision–making process. They are related to each other. We cannot ignore the importance of both of financial accounting and management.

Finacial Management and Cost Accounting: Cost Accounting and Financial Management are concerned with large organization. Generally, large and big industrial houses will have a separate cost accounting department. Cost accounting is a system for arriving at accurate cost of production of a product. Cost accounting is a subject for ascertaining and recording of financial affairs related to a particular product. The information related to various costs and in various stages is extremely useful for financial manager for control of business. Hence, the financial manager is related with better utilization of funds while cost accountant is concerned with operation cost of the firm. Therefore, the cost accounting provides information to control the business activities of the commercial enterprise.

Financial Management and Asset Management: Asset Management and Financial Management is another important area of management. Assets are most important resources for conducting business of a commercial enterprise. Assets are resources that are more valuable and they need careful monitoring. Assets are tangible in monitory value, which reflects appreciation or depreciation from time to time. Assets may be classified as fixed and current assets. Another classification of assets is tangible and intangible assets. Assets further classified as moveable and immovable assets. However, the assets must be properly used and should be looking after by the financial manager. Financial management is concerned with acquisisition and proper maintenance of assets. It is necessary for a business enterprise to have a mix of assets for achieving the firm's goal.

Financial Management and Marketing Management: Marketing management and financial management are another area of interest in management. Marketing is one of the emerging subjects in functional area of management. Marketing is useful for selling the products to the consumer. The success and failure of a company depends upon the marketing capability. *Marketing* is based on customer needs, desires, and convenience of the customer in this digital era a high quality product needs a good marketing strategy. If the firm does not have any marketing schemes, the products may not be sold in the market. The success of a product is based on price, quality, and advertisement. Advertising is a part of marketing management. Marketing management is a combination of different aspects such as *Pricing Policy, Product Mix Demand Assessement Competitive Strategy*. The marketing manager is closely related with all these aspects. He provides information to the finance manager for taking a joint decision. He will inform about the price changes in the market demand and supply of commodities, competitive position in the market, and movement about competitor, all of these information procured and collected by the marketing manager. The information will be transmitted to the financial manager. Full information about these aspects will make financial manager to take a reasonable decision. A strong and reasonable decision will definitely stimulate the profitability of a commercial enterprise.

Financial Management and Personnel Management: Personnel management and financial management are one of the areas of the management. The personnel management is related with management of human resources. Financial management is concerned with management of monetary valuable items. Both of them are managing resources. Human resource management is a highly complex and complicated area. Personnel management is involved with a recruitment, training, and placement of staff. All these activities will be carried out with the help of financial management. The total labour requirement of a company will be prepared by the HR manager and transmitted to the financial manager. In practice, the financial manager will have dealt with all departments in the organization. He should examine and analyze the various possibilities to take and implement a decision. If the company's financial position is very critical then he may curb the expenditure with the approval of top-level management. If the firm's financial position is very strong and fat resources, he may give flexibility and liberty to all other areas of management. The financial manager will be happy if plenty of resources will be available.

Functions of Financial Management: Financial management is a dynamic subject and it changes very fastly. It deals with aspects of each department of organization.

The financial management is an extremely practical and utilitarian subject. It is mostly useful in day-to-day administration of financial affairs of the business enterprise. It is closely associated with action and reaction of financial affairs of the company. The modern finance theories are widely used by finance managers, bankers, investors, and mutual fund operators. It is closely related with Indian financial system. *Indian Financial System* is a highly dynamic aspect of economic system. It is generated and procured from economics. Hence, there is a relation between economics and financial management. It is derived from economics. It is separated from economics and fully developed as one of the functional area of management. Indian financial system is concerned about money, credit, and finance. A well-developed financial system can influence the economic development. The Indian financial system is a combination of different aspects. It consists of,

(a) Financial Markets
(b) Financial Services
(c) Financial Institutions
(d) Financial Instruments

Every business organization in India should rotate in the economic system. The economic system contains business and socio-political environment. The corporate sector must operate in macro level economic policy. The Government prepares the economic policy. Hence, there is a strong relation between Government and industry. Policy is a long-term strategy. If a Government prepares a policy, it should be stick on to that decision. The corporate sector in India will rotate in broad policies of Government. The socio-political environment consists with the population, trade unionism, consumerism, political intervention in business operations.

However, the modern finance manager should work to achieve the desired goals of the firm. The functional area of financial management has been organized into three specific areas. 1. Planning policies and decisions, 2. Funds Management, 3. Control and Information.

PLANNING POLICIES AND DECISIONS

Planning is an important function in management. A proper planning is necessary for achieving the desired goal. Planning means an advanced course of action. Planning is a scientific investigation process related to various complex decisions. Planning can be made for long-term or short-term. It is a continuous process. Planning is a steering to vehicle. Planning is a proper sense of direction. Planning is related to all aspects of the organization. Planning is a course of all advance action. It takes into consideration of all activities of the organization. Generally, long-term planning involves 3 to 5 years. Planning compels top-level management to think ahead. The most important financial policies and decisions are presented below:

Financial Policies and Decisions

Long-term	*Short-term*
Strategic Decisions	Operational Decisions
Capital Structure	Manufacturing
Dividend Policy	Marketing
Growth Policy	Personnel Research and Development

Funds management; Financial management occupies an important role in functional area of management. The Modern financial management has come a long way from the traditional corporate finance. Now the finance manager is working in a challenging environment. In this situation funds management is an important function of a financial management. It deals with mobilization and proper utilization of funds. The efficiency of a business enterprise depends upon better utilization of resources. The corporate sector usually raises funds from market on either long-term or short-term resources. The management of funds involves two aspects is presented below:

Management of Funds

Mobilisation of Funds	*Utilisation of Funds*
(a) Quantum	(a) Fixed Assets (capital expenditure)
(b) Source	(b) Working Capital (current operating needs)
(c) Cost	(c) Investments (surplus funds)
(d) Time	

Mobilisation of Funds is one of the important functions of financial management. Financial resources are necessary for any kind of business enterprise. Raising of financial resources from the market is a highly specialized activity. Usually companies will raise the resources on long and short-term basis. The long-term resources of the funds through equity, debentures, and term loans from financial institutions. Short-term loans of finance can be raised from banks for working capital purpose. The short-term loans are generally related to below one year. The short-term needs are met by bridge loans from financial institutions and from associate companies. The medium term sources of finance can also be procured from market by issue of convertible debentures, inviting fixed deposits, from public with 2 to 3 years maturity. All the mobilization of resources made from the market attracts cost. The financial resources are available to the corporate sector in different rates of interest from time to time. However, the aim of the financial management is to provide the resources at the lowest cost of funds. Therefore, the financial manager should take a careful decision regarding average cost. Fund should be kept as low as possible. The cost of funds adversely affect on profitability of the corporate sector. Hence, the financial manager always thinks about the reduced level of cost of funds. The financial manager may think about a good blend of mix debt and equity. Debt equity is a combination of own fund and borrowed fund. The mix should be a balanced factor. If debt is disproportionate to the equity, it involves high interest burden and repayment. A business activity should not be starved for want of timely and adequate cash. A chronic cash shortage may lead to insolvency.

Utilization of Funds: Financial management involves for proper utilization of funds. After mobilization of funds from the market at the right source, at the right cost, at the right time, should be used in a proper way. Otherwise, the entire skills applied by the financial manager will go to a wasteful exercise. The financial management always thinks about better utilization of funds. It reveals that long-term funds are meant for financing fixed assets and short-term funds as working capital.

Control and Information: Control is another important function of financial management. It is interlinked with planning. Planning is an advanced course of action. Budget is part of planning. Budget is a document, which based on expenses and revenue. Expenses are necessary for any kind of business enterprise. Every company should prepare its own budget as part of their planning...Budget is consisted with target and achievement. Target is based on prediction. Accurate prediction is the efficiency of top-level management. Managerial efficiency is a combination of different kinds of experts.

Therefore, the budget preparation is an important task before management. It creates a proper organizational climate for systematic growth of the business enterprise. In addition to all these activities, several operational controls are also required in the routine life of the management. Management of money, men, material, and machines is an important task before the administration. For better functioning of organization, the corporate sector should apply several control techniques.... All these action and reaction of affairs should be intimated to the management in timely. Timely supply of suitable information system is vital for the success of any organization.

Role of Financial Manager: After liberalization, globalization, and privatization the entire corporate sector has been changed drastically. A good environment has been created for the development of industrial houses. The Government policies have been fuelled the growth of corporate sector tremendously. A drastic change in economy created a lot of opportunities to the 'corporate sector.' Interest rates, deregulated, convertibility of rupee, foreign direct investment limits, entry of private sector into new horizons' all these factors has been helped to the speedy industrialization of digital India. India is becoming a leader in knowledge management... Hence, the role of financial manager is changed and occupied a key position. He is one of the dynamic member of managerial team. The emerging development of new financial system, financial services industry, financial tools, techniques, instruments, products, recent innovations, have all changed the role of a finance manager.

Place of Financial Management in the Corporate Sector: Finance is one of the important function in all industrial houses. It occupies a major place in the organization, which cannot be ignored. The top-level management is related to prepare financial policy of the company. The managing director and the board of directors will collectively take a decision regarding financial aspects. An important officer who will be known as financial controller will assist the higher-level capacity team. Financial controller occupies a crucial role in assisting the management team. He enables the management group to make good financial decision and try to impose financial discipline in the organization. The efficiency of the financial controller will be reflected in the form of high liquidity position with high profitability. He will be an important and influencing person to maintain good financial relations with others. Broadly speaking a finance manager may be known as financial controller, vice-president, (finance), chief accountant and treasurer. All of these various positions will carry same prime responsibility of performing the finance function. The place of finance department in a large organization has been presented below:

Board of Directors

	President	
Vice Presidnet Production	*Vice President Finance*	*Vice President Sales*
Treasurer		*Controller*
Credit Management Cash Management Banking Relations Portfolio Management		Accountant Taxes Audit Bugeting

ORGANISATION CHART OF FINANCE FUNCTION

The managing director is the supreme authority in the corporate world. He keeps the board of directors with latest information in all aspects occurring in the company. The chief executive of the finance wing will directly works under the control of managing director or president of the company. He will submit the full information regarding financial aspects of the organization to the managing director. He may have many offices and executives under him to carry out his functional channels very smoothly. His functions can be divided into two methods, (a) treasurer, (b) controller. As a function of treasurer, he may involve cash, bank, and portfolio management. These activities occupy a significant role in the determination of corporate financial policy. The controller area function involves keeping of financial affairs of the company from time to time. Budgeting and auditing occupies important aspects in policy framing of the corporate sector. In a resources constraint situation the financial management aspects cannot be ignored. Financial strategies are needed for every company to face financial crunch. The market is combination of different aspects and involving many problems such as demand and supply position of raw material, labour problems, obsolesce of technology etc., However, efficient functioning of financial management will be reflected in maintenance of solvency which built a strong goodwill in the business environment. The finance manager has to help in taking decisions in the aspects of investment, financing, and dividend. A good financial design will diffidently boost the revenues to the firm. The asset mix is the barometer of an efficiency related to financial expert. The finance expert will have to deal with capital market. He should fully understand the various aspects of the capital market. The finance manager should know about the business environment and financial system. Financial system is a combination of different elements of the economy. It is the part of the economy. A strong economy needs a good financial system. A system is a set of interrelated parts working together to achieve the goal. Financial system includes the complex of institutions and mechanism for investment. It is closely related to savings and expenditure process of a community or a nation. The finance manager should thoroughly know about the Indian financial system, which helps to take right decisions at right time. The system reveals the supply and demand position of the capital. It involves the study of fund facilitating institutions, and helpful to the policy-framers to take decisions. The financial system was become more dynamic after introduction of new economic policy in 1991. The policy has completely changed the Indian economy. The traditional system has been changed and a new model approach look takes the digital economy. Indian financial system is based on four important pillars, (a) financial markets, (b) financial institutions, (c) financial services, (d) financial assets.

The development of a nation depends upon these elements. The Indian economy is based on a strong growth of gross domestic product. *The Growth in GDP* reveals the financial status of the country. A strong growth is only possible with the development of these four elements. The Government of India is continuously making efforts to develop these elements in tune with the new economic policy, 1991. However, the poverty is main problem where India struggling since Independence. Poverty will attack with knowledge management. India is a country with vast potential human resources than any nation in the world. Poverty will be eliminated with a committed patriotism in all spheres of the society. Politicians, bureaucrats, entrepreneurs, economist, farmers, scientist, academicians should change their mindset towards achieving the goal. Financial Markets are related to various elements such as money market, capital market. Money market is associated with providing short-term loans to borrowers. Capital market is involved in provision of long-term capital to the industrial houses. It is further categorized as *Primary Market and Secondary Market.* Financial market is good infrastructure for development.

Financial Institutions are another important aspect in the system. It closely associated with the observations of banking and non-banking institutions. It studies about the policy-making organization central bank. The R.B.I. is India's Central Bank, which takes all decisions with the guidance from the Union Government. Banking sector comprises with the study of R.B.I., commercial banks, cooperative banks, urban cooperative banks, post office savings banks. Non-Banking sector consists of with provident fund, small saving organizations, *UTI, LIC, GIC, Investment Companies, Mutual Funds,* Investment trust, housing development finance companies, national housing bank, venture capital, and HUDCO. All these institutions are functioning with guidance from GoI. Financial services are another important factor in the financial system. It facilitates and acts as a coordinator between borrowers and lenders. It is necessary for the development of industry. The industrialization process is depended upon its efficiency. It can be further classified as fee and fund based. It occupies a dominant role in the formation of capital in the country. No one can ignore its importance in process of newly established units. It provides excellent services to the new entrants in the market. It also provides good opportunity to savers for better return of their investment. Return is a reward to the investor. He always searches for the sources of better return alternatives. Therefore, the financial services provide a way for higher return sources to the common investor. India has strong savings potential, which may be diverted towards capital formation. A growth in capital formation is a good indicator for the improvement of financial status of the country. For this purpose, the GoI made drastic reforms to protect the investor's confidence. The Union Government was enacted various laws for the good environment of business. Companies act, securities contracts regulation act, capital issues act, and various legislations had been introduced for imposing discipline in the business environment. Hence, the modern financial manager of the corporate sector should be well equipped with all aspects of the investment climate of the country. A finance manager is now responsible for shaping the fortunes of the business concern and is involved in the most important decisions like merger, acquisitions e.g. He has to take many decisions as financial controller, vice–president, chief accountant and treasurer etc.

Importance of Financial Management: Any kind of the business organization cannot be ignored the importance of financial management. Finance is provision of money when at required. A good financial management of the company will show impact on business concern. A sound financial management is necessary for profit and non-profit organizations. The financial manager's efficiency can be measured through various sources, such as deployment of funds in fixed and in working capital. He has to work on debt equity ratio; cost of capital, return on capital, etc. He helps in making profit not only at present but also in future. He should take care of entire business enterprise. Financial management occupied a dominant role in profit planning, controlling, inventories, and costs. It helps in optimizing the output for a given input of financial resources.

Financial Forecasting: Forecasting means prediction about a certain events. Financial forecasting refers to the formal process of prediction of future events. It determines in advance requirement and utilization of funds for a future period. An accurate estimation of funds inflow and outflow creates a strong and stable working environment in the business. It is a systematic and scientific way of approach to assets the future things. It is an advanced technique of procurement and utilization of funds. It is a good technique of systematic presentation of data. The data will be in the form of financial statements and ratios. Prediction is necessary in business environment. A strong and accurate prediction will get success in the achievement of desired goal. Forecasting is the part of planning process. A good planning will give results in a highly business competitive environment. Forecasting techniques provides immense utility for a business organization. They provide adequate information for financial decision-making. They have provided an opportunity to plan for firm's growth and financial needs. The forecasting technique is sales method, regression and multiple regression method. Sales are the most important element for a commercial enterprise. It is the simplest forecasting technique method. It is popularly known as percentage of sales method. Sales occupy a dominant role in financial needs of a business enterprise. Therefore, assets and liabilities, revenues and expenses can be expressed as a percentage of sales. It is useful for short-term forecasting. Financial information can be developed for projected sales at different levels. Another important technique is known as simple regression method. It reveals past relationship between sales and various aspects, a regression line can be drawn. It is related with sales and is item at a time. The company can make projections with the change in sales levels. Multiple regression method is another technique where sales are related to various variables. It is a good technique for computation of the amount of different items. A financial analyst may adopt techniques as per his situation. Any kind of technique can be used as per the availability of data and the purpose of forecasting. Financial forecasting is more useful to prepare various statements such as proforma income statement and proforma balance sheet, proforma funds flow statement and cash budgeting. All these statements are useful in making of financial decisions. They reveal the financial status and financial position of the business concern.

Financial Planning: Profit is the inner element of any kind of business enterprise. The earning profit capacity reveals efficiency of a business concern. The firm should be able to achieve its objectives by utilizing its resources in a proper way. A business concern can achieve its goal by adopting a systematic approach, known as "financial planning". Financial planning is necessary for all business concerns. Planning is an advanced course of action to achieve goal. It reveals the companies growth, performance, investments, and requirement of funds. Plans will be prepared for a given certain period. Generally, all companies will prepare financial plans for 3 to 5 years. It indicates the process of various financial statements such as *Projected Profit and Loss Account, Balance Sheet and Funds Flow Statement*.

Commercial enterprises will stay in the market, until earnings of profits. Growth in sales is an important element in survival. A strong growth in a sales creates a stability of the firm. The market share occupied by a commercial enterprise indicates the efficiency of a concern. In business, a historical events may not occur in the future. Financial planning involves various steps in careful analysis of past performance, market position, investment strategies, cash flow, and stability. It can be described as a tool for the future. It involves estimation of future funds requirement and the way of raising resources from different financial instruments. It focuses on investment decisions. It is based on financial policy. Financial policy is related with its corporate strategy. Strategy is a fundamental pattern of present and resources development. Strategy can be seen as influences on the firm's effectiveness and efficiency. Financial manager has two objectives: (a) maximization of the wealth of shareholders, (b) raising of resources at lower cost. Financial goals of a commercial enterprise can be described as maximizing the levels, profitability, and growth. Financial management always think about to enhance the present levels of 'Book Value of Networth, market value of per share, cash flow per share and operating profit. It has another aspect to enhance the levels of price earning ratio return on investment net profit to net worth, net profit, net profit margin market share'. However, the basic objective of the financial management is to achieve growth in 'EPS Total Assets, Sales'. Financial goals are the quantititative expression of a business enterprise mission and strategy. The financial priorities will change according to the changes in the business environment. A demand and supply for a fund requirement of a business enterprise is a continuous balancing act of a company's financial policy. Therefore, financial goals are changeable and unstable. It depends upon many factors.

The funds requirement and financing decisions are two major areas of financial decision-making. Generally, every business organization will prepare an estimation of future funds requirement decision. The firm will assess the total funds requirement keeping in view of long-term needs. Financing decision is related to raise the funds through a low cost fund segment. Therefore, the top-level management will take care of all these aspects. Financial plan involves—(a) for estimation of funds, (b) combination of different kinds of financial instruments, (c) implementation process of funds administration. Therefore, a good financial planning helps the firm to achieve the goal. It is necessary for any firm to monitor better utilization of financial resources. The financial plan will determine the quantum of finance, mix of financial assets and flotation time from market. A good financial plan has the following principles:

(a) Easy understanding
(b) Future-oriented
(c) Visualization
(d) Utilization
(e) Unforeseen
(f) Solvency
(g) Savings

A good financial plan should easily understandable by investing public. The plan should contain a simplified financial structure. The structure should be easily manageable. It determines the types of securities to be raised, at what interest rate and sources. It should not create complications.

A good financial plan will reflect future ambitions. The plan would continue to operate for a long period. The firms usually do the business with high spirit and a strong desire to reach higher level of sales. Hence, the need of finance may arise at any time. The promoters should be not in deviation from the original plan may destroy all aspects of business organization.

A good financial plan shall play a vital role in the decision-making process. It may contain accurate forecasting of the business needs. The plan can adopt future technological improvement, demand forecasting, and scale of changes in production. All aspects regarding business environment will be undertaken while drafting a financial plan.

A good financial plan monitors better utilization of financial resources. The plan should constitute all genuine needs of the firm. The firm should not be in a financial crisis environment. It should maintain a close relationship with the short and long-term needs of the company. A proper utilization of resources may generate better yields. A low cost of sources of fund may bring cheerful movements to the shareholders. A strong growth in sales will stimulate the profitability of the corporate house.

A good financial plan will have to face unforeseen situation in business environment. A well-designed plan can absorb all situations and move without any interruption in business activities. A stable financial plan provides the way to all aspects of the business environment. It provides solutions, when capital lies in idle position. It reduces the risk and stimulates the profits. All contingencies will be expected in advance and precautions and changes will be made as per isolation and expectations.

Solvency is the most important for any business enterprise. It reflects the liquid position of the firm. Ability to pay debt within stipulated time is an important character in the market. Confidence in the market in a highly competitive environment is must for a developing company. A good financial plan shall provide a provision for money when it required. Flexibility is another important aspect in maintenance of liquidity. Liquidity and profitability is the oxygen of a commercial enterprise.

Savings is another important element in preparation of a good financial plan. The plan should be made with low cost of sources of funds available in the market. The cost of raising resources and interest burden should be kept in mind while drafting a plan. The plan always show the way of economy in the form of revenue expenditure. Economy in the plan should be reflected in order to increase profit volumes to patronize the shareholders.

Financial goal of the firm will be achieved through a good financial plan. The following elements constitue the financial plan:

1. Capital
2. Capitalisation

(1) *Capital:* Capital means money with which a business is started. Every business needs money to start, operate and expansion. Money earns money. In business, the money circulation is more important. The requirement of money by a business enterprise depends upon business environment. Usually all business firms' needs money for their short-term and long-term tenure. Therefore, a business enterprise needs money in two kinds. They are fixed capital and working capital.

Fixed capital is helpful to a firm to meet long-term needs. It is essential for any kind of business enterprise. It occupies an important role while the company is in formation stage. At the initial stage of the firm, it is oxygen and used for speedy completion of all construction and formalities work. It is used for acquisition of tangible and intangible assets. The company through issues of equity and debentures can procure it. The requirement of fixed capital depends upon several factors.

1. Business Environment
2. Quantum of Credit
3. Acquisition of Asset
4. Kind of Product

Business environment occupies a dominant role in determination of amount of fixed capital. All business enterprises rotate in business environment. There are various kinds of businesses exists in the economy. Some kind of business require higher amount of fixed capital. For ex-railways and electric companies, water supply systems. Public utilities needs greater amount of fixed capital. All of these organizations need heavy investment at initial stage of commencing projects. At the same time, trading for commodities needs a small amount of fixed capital.

Quantum of Trade is another important factor in assessment of fixed capital. Generally, large industries need a greater amount of fixed capital. Manufacturing organizations usually require a high component of fixed capital. They involve higher amount of expenditure for purchasing of capital assets. Industrial products heavy machinery equipment, units requires higher amount of initial investment.

Acquisition of Asset: Acquisition of asset is one of the influencing factor for higher amount of investment. Generally, companies either purchase capital asset or go for leasing and hire purchase. Hire purchase and leasing system will involve a lower amount of capital. If the company wishes to purchase the assets then the situation, demands higher amount of capital. Hence, the requirement of capital depends upon the policy.

Kind of Product: The nature of the product determines the requirement of the fixed capital. Generally, manufacturing of the consumer utilities like oil, soaps, cosmetics, will require a small amount of fixed capital. Manufacturing of white goods, home appliances, heavy machinery, and automobiles industrial goods needs capital that is more fixed.

The fixed capital is an initial investment of commercial enterprises. It should be raised at minimum cost. It may not be refundable. It requires a continuous recurring expenditure. It should be utilized more effectively. A greater impact will show on its earning. It is seed money of business enterprise. Management of fixed capital depends upon several factors, (a) It is necessary to utilize the fixed capital for increasing of its earning capacity, (b) It is better to acquire assets on hire purchase or leasing basis, (c) It is better to acquire machinery with latest technology and equipment, (d) It is better to avoid idle capacity of machinery, (e) it is a better to take care about the maintenance of machinery. The assets must be maintained properly and periodical inspection, overhauling repairs is necessary. All these activities remove the hurdles in achieving higher productivity, (f) It is better to provide proper depreciation on assets to enable the firm for timely replacement, (g) It is better to procure fixed capital through a good financial instrument, (h) A well-designed capital structure will show a greater impact on earnings.

Therefore, management of fixed capital is a very delicate. Financial issue, which shows internal asset on long-term basis. It can be raised from the following sources:

(a) Shares
(b) Debentures

Share Capital: Finance is the lifeblood of a commercial enterprise. The source of finance depends upon requirement of needs of the business. Financial resources provide more productivity to achieve desired goals. The requirement of finance for a business enterprise depends upon time basis. The money is needed by a business in two situations long and short-term period. The requirement of finance for more than 5 years is known as long-term finance. Short-term finance is a provision of money for 1-year period. Ownership capital is the best sources of long-term finance. Issue of the shares is the most common and popular method of rising long-term funds. Share is a small piece of monetary valuable unit. Share is defined "a share is the share in the capital of a company and includes stock except where a distinction between stock and share is expressed or implied".

Section 2 (46) Companies Act, 1956

The companies issue shares to the public. The buyers of the share are known as shareholders. They are entitled to get dividend. Dividend is a reward to the investors. They occupy a dominant role in the management. They can participate and vote in all meetings of the company. Usually shares can be categorized in two kinds. A. Equity, B. Preference. Equity shares are becoming more popular at present. They are real owners of the company. It is the best source of permanent capital. It costs very low. The buyers of the equity shares are known as equity shareholders. They can bear risk. They take active part in management of the company. Not all shareholders of the company can run the business affairs. Hence, they nominate some of the members to manage the affairs. The nominated are elected members is known as directors. The Board of Directors constitutes top-level management, chair, directors, managing director are shareholders. The company management depends upon the democratic system. Shareholders will elect directors. Directors select chair, managing director and other persons. Equity shareholders will get dividend in tune with the company earnings. They get higher rate of dividend, if company generates hefty profits. If the company fails to get the profits, they will not be paid dividends. However, the equity has advantages and disadvantages which are presented below:

Advantages:

Equity share capital provides the following advantages to the corporate sector:

(a) Low cost of permanent financial resources.
(b) Repayable only on the winding up of a company.
(c) No pressure on financial cost.
(d) Additional financial resources can be raised through rights issues.
(e) No charge or pledge on assets of the company.

Disadvantages:

(a) Dividend payment is not treated as business expenses for tax purpose.
(b) Satisfying equity shareholders is a adventurous task before the company management.
(c) There will be always conflict between personal interest and company interest.
(d) There will be scope for manipulations in the company management.
(e) The cost rising for equity fund is very high in relation to debt and preference shares.
(f) Excessive reliance on equity may cause to over capitalization.
(g) There will be always confiict between senior and junior shareholders.

Preference Shares: Preference shares are one of the sources of finance for corporate sector. They are issued by public limited companies. The preference shareholders will get a fixed amount of dividend on their investment. They carry preferential rights than equity shareholders. They are entitled to get dividend in advance to equity shareholders. They may be paid share amount in advance to equity shareholders. At the winding up of the company, they get their capital earlier than equity shareholders do. Therefore, they get some preference than equity shareholders. They have some priority than other class of shareholders. Actually speaking they are not the real owners of the company. They are only fund suppliers to the corporate sector. Dividend payment is not obligation. The shareholders will have no right to demand for the dividend. The dividend payment authority lies with the Board of Directors. The financial resources raised through issue of preference shares are more cheap sources for the corporate sector. It is best and cheap sources of finance available to the corporate sector. It is a permanent capital lying in the company. They do not require any sort of charge against assets of the company. The dividend paid by the corporate sector will not attract income tax exemption as business expenditure. The amount of interest paid will be treated as business expenditure by the income tax act. They dilute the claims of equity shareholders over the assets of the company. If the company pays a regular dividend even in declining profits environment leads to insolvency. Preference shares can be categorized as follows:

(a) Cumulative preference shares
(b) Non-cumulative preference shares
(c) Participative preference shares
(d) Non-participative preference shares
(e) Redeemable and Irredeemable preference shares

Cumulative Preference Shares means, the shareholders will get dividend regularly. If the company is unable to pay in a particular period, their dividend will be paid in future. The company will pay in arrears of dividend when the company earns sufficient profits. Hence, they will get dividend continuously.

Non-cumulative Preference Shareholders are not entitled to claim arrears. They have no right to claim dividend. If in a particular period the company fails to earn sufficient profits their dividend will be lapsed. Dividend will not be carry forward to the next year.

Participative Preference Shareholers are entitled to get their dividend as usual. If the company having surplus profits after payment of equity shareholders dividend again enjoy the additional dividend from the available surplus profit.

Non-participating Preference Shareholers do not have right to enjoy the dividends from the surplus profit. They will get a fixed rate of dividend at once per year.

Redeemable Preference Shares can be redeemable capital amount during the lifetime of a company. The company will refund these shares. The date of redeemable period will also be announced while at the time of issue of such kind of shares.

Irredeemable Preference Share capital can be refunded their capital amount only at the time of liquidation.

However, at present there is no popularity for these shares. After introduction of economic reforms, there is greater demand for equity capital. In India, equity culture has been increasing exponentially. Further reforms may stimulate the savings from the public.

Working Capital is useful to run the business organizations without interruption in production. The day-to-day operations of a commercial enterprise involves a series of regular payments. Business organizations require paying expenses regularly. It requires paying daily wages to meet factory-running expenses, to pay suppliers, for supply of raw materials, etc. Hence, all payments will be made from a pool amount known as working capital. A corpus fund should be created to meet all day-to-day expenses. The goodwill depends upon timely payment of cash to various parties involved in the market. A prompt payment stimulates the image of a business enterprise. Generally, sales do no yield cash immediately from the market. In this situation, the working capital exists to settle all the payments. Working capital means excess of current assets over current liabilities. The company management should take a proper care about working capital. The management of working capital in a good manner leads to smooth functioning of all activities. Mismanagement of current assets can be costly. It leads to show effect on productivity. Hence, the management should take proper estimation of the working capital requirement. A good estimation leads to sufficient provision of money. Inadequate funds will result low amount of profits. hence however, the requirement of working capital depends upon the following factors:

(a) Production strategy
(b) Business transaction
(c) Work process
(d) Credit policy
(e) Turnover
(f) Fluctuations
(g) Availability of raw material

Production Strategy is one of the important factors, which determine the requirement of working capital. A large quantity of inventory influences the amount of working capital. Mechanization and automation will have effect on working capital requirements. Manual process of manufacturing requires higher amount of working capital. Production schedules of the company determine the quantum of working capital.

Business Transactions occupy an important role in assessment of working capital. The transactions are depend upon the nature of the business. Generally, public utilities organizations have a lower level of working capital. These organizations will have cash transactions. There is no credit transactions like railways, electricity, gas, fuel, etc., they require low inventory with high turnover. General manufacturing and trading organizations requires a large amount of money for working capital.

Work Process is another influencing factor for assessment of working capital. A lengthy process of manufacturing organizations requires a higher amount of working capital. Capital-intensive organizations needs large amount of working capital to maintain sophisticated machines.

Credit Policy is one of the important and influencing factors in determination of working capital. A liberal credit to intermediaries needs higher amount of working capital. A company, which enjoys a liberal credit from its suppliers, require lower amount of working capital. A company follows strict credit norms will show impact on lower amount of working capital. A strict credit policy followed by suppliers require higher amount of working capital.

Turnover is also one of the influencing factors in determining working capital. The need of working capital depends upon the sales turnover. The velocity of the turnover influences the requirement of the working capital. A higher rate of sales turnover leads to lower amount of working capital. A lower level of sales turnover causes higher amount of working capital.

Fluctuations are necessary in any business. Seasonal business creates fluctuations. Generally, some goods are available in a particular season. In this juncture, it needs more working capital than the rest of the period.

Supply of Raw Material occupies an important factor in assessment of working capital. Generally, business organizations needs large reserves of raw material due to irregular sales and interrupted supply. A scared raw material requires need to maintain large inventory. In this position, it requires higher amount of working capital.

All of the above factors influence the level of working capital. Finance is a scared commodity. It should be used for maximization of shareholder's wealth. The basic aim of the financial management is to provide better returns to the shareholders. Sales do not yield cash immediately. There is always a time gap between sale and receipt of cash. There are two concepts of working capital.

(a) Gross Working Capital
(b) Networking Capital

Gross Working Capital is related to overall firm's investment in current assets. Current asset means the assets, which are easily convertible into cash within one accounting year. Current assets include debtors, accounts receivables, book debts, bills receivables, and stock. Net working capital has been defined as difference between current assets and current liabilities. Current liabilities means the claims to be payable by the firm within one accounting year. The claims which belongs to outsiders should be payable on request. Current liabilities include creditors, bills payable, accounts payable and outstanding expenses. Net working capital further can be categorized as positive working capital and negative working capital. A positive working capital arises when current assets exceed current liabilities. In other words, the value of current assets should be more than the worth of current liabilities. A negative working capital arises when the current liabilities exceeds current assets. In other words, current liabilities dominate the current assets. Hence, the firm should be careful in two elements, excessive and inadequate level of working capital resources. However, investment in current assets should be kept adequate level for the smooth functioning of manufacturing process without interruption. At the same time, the firm should also take proper care about excessive investment in current asset. Excessive investment leads to idle investment. Idle investment earns nothing. Inadequate fund threaten solvency of the firm. Hence, the firm should always keep in mind about the working capital fund. The needs of business fluctuate in the business environment. This situation may lead excess or shortage of working capital frequently. Therefore, the finance manager should know and have knowledge of the sources of the working capital funds. Networking capital is a qualitative aspect. It is barometer for measuring liquidity position of the firm. The working capital may be financed by permanent sources of funds. It depends upon the operating cycle of a business. It is better to maintain current assets at higher level than current liabilities. The current assets level must be kept twice to current liabilities. The firm should maintain the quality of current assets continuously. A weak liquidity position threaten solvency of the firm. This position is unsafe and unsound. Mismanagement of current assets leads to uncertainty. A good financial manager always takes prompt and timely action for improving and corrects the imbalances in the liquidity position of the firm. It indicates the judicious mix of long and short-term funds for financing. The management of the company must decide the extent of source of finance by issues of shares and debentures. The basic objective of financial management is to maximize the shareholders wealth. A good working capital management leads to earn sufficient profits. The amount of such profits depends upon the magnitude of sales. Sale is the most important and influencing factor for survival of a business firms. These activities should be halt for lack of working capital fund. Manufacturing organization needs the following events:

(a) Purchase of Raw Material (Cash from WC Fund)
(b) Work in Process (Material+Labour)
(c) Finished Product (Final Product)
(d) Accounts Receivables (Credit Sales)
(e) Cash

CASH RAW MATERIAL WIP (WORK IN PROCESS)
FINISHED GOODS ACCOUNTS RECEIVABLE CASH

The above events will be repeated repeatedly in the life of a business enterprise.

Operating Cycle contains a series of number of events. It constitutes an important factor in assessment of adequate working capital needs. A right prediction of working capital depends upon the operating cycle. Operating cycle is a time duration element. The time gap between sale of goods and yield of cash is known as operating cycle. Cash inflow and outflow is the most important and influencing factor in survival of the firm in market. The best management of the funds provides good results. It leads to uninterrupted functioning of a firm. The conversion period influences the requirement of working capital amount. The conversion period is high, the firm is required to mobilize higher amount of working capital. There are three conversion periods in all manufacturing periods.

1. Inventory Conversion
2. Debtors Conversion

Inventory Conversion refers to that total time required for producing and selling of the final commodity. It is a combination of raw material work in process conversion period and finished commodity conversion period.

Operating Cycle= Raw Material Conversion Period +Work in Process Conversion Model+Finished Commodity Conversion Period

$$OP = R + W + F$$

The Operating cycle can be categorized into two ways (a) gross operating cycle, (b) net operating cycle. Gross operating cycle is referred as the total of inventory conversion period and debtor's conversion period. Net operating cycle means, the time gap between cash collections from sale and cash payment for resources. It is also known as cash conversion cycle. Depreciation and profit should be excluded in computation of cash conversion cycle. A good management of cash inflow and outflow yield better results in the corporate sector. The basic aim of the financial management will be fulfilled by good management techniques of working capital.

Types of Working Capital: Profit maximization and wealth maximization is the fundamental desire of financial management in order to serve more welfare to the shareholders. Shareholders welfare is the top priority before the company management. It will be provided in various methods. A good provision of working capital leads to get more profits in order to satisfy shareholder's desire. The top-level management should think about provision of working capital sufficiently. Adequate provision of working capital generates higher levels of production without any interruptions. Therefore, working capital influences the productivity levels of a commercial enterprise. It can be divided into two categories.

(a) Permanent Working Capital
(b) Temporary Working Capital

(a) *Parmenent Working Capital*: Permanent working capital is the most important and influencing factor in achieving minimum levels of production activities for the entire year. The company should maintain current assets levels on a continuous basis over 24+7+365 days. Permanent working capital is also known as "Core Current Assets." Adequate level of provision of working capital enables the organization to carry out production activities very smoothly and efficiently. The provision of working capital fund may not be returned to the suppliers of fund during the lifetime of the company. Therefore, it is better to raise funds for working capital on permanent basis through issue of equity shares. Equity shares are the best sources of provision for permanent capital. If the company introduces permanent working capital, it may not be possible to return the same to the fund suppliers. The quantum of amount of permanent working capital should be increased to the extent of growth in business operations. If the company achieves higher level of growth, the permanent working capital should also be increased.

(b) *Temporary Working Capital*: Temporary working capital is a provision to meet business fluctuations from time-to-time basis. It represents an additional amount of fund to meet unexpected demand of the market. Business is a combination of risk and return. The firm does not know when an additional orders knocking the doors. Hence, the firm should be prepared for a provision of temporary working capital fund. The fund suppliers of temporary working capital may be returned to them within a stipulated period. The company should make a plan to refund the temporary working capital during the off-season period. It can be procured from short-term finance. It may be refunded within one-year period. Bank credit is best alternative sources for financing temporary working capital. It is a fluctuating provision. The requirement of higher level of temporary working capital may yield better result. It is also known as extra working capital.

Balanced Level of Working Capital: Every business organization should maintain permanent and temporary working capital in order to achieve the desired goals. A good design of provision of working capital stimulates higher profitability of the firm. Hence, the firm should maintain a balanced position to achieve the goal of a firm. It should have adequate working capital. Shortage of working capital may causes low productivity with high cost. Excessive provision of working capital may leads to arise idle fund. Idle fund earns nothing. Excessive working capital is harmful to the business organization in several ways. It results over procurement of inventory levels. The situation arises to pay additional maintenance expenditure. There is a scope for wastage, theft, and fluctuations in price levels of inventory. Excessive working capital leads to arise of bad debts due to negligence in collection of credit sales. The higher incidence of bad debts adversely affects the profits. Excessive working capital paves the way for increasing management inefficiency. Accumulation of higher inventory levels creates to earn speculative profits heftily. A higher level of profits tends to announce liberal dividends, which may not be possible in future. Speculative profits are not stable and baseless growth. Shortage of working capital is also harmful to the business enterprise in several ways.

(a) It reduces the earning capacity of a firm.
(b) It unable the firm to avail attractive credit opportunities.
(c) It unable the firm to pay short-term obligations which leads to damage for goodwill of the firm.
(d) It is not possible for the top-level management to run a firm with continuous financial problems.
(e) It leads to increase operating inefficiency of the firm to meet day-to-day operations.
(f) A continuous financial problems leads to ignore the maintenance of fixed assets.

Therefore, the adequate level of working capital is necessary for efficient management of the firm. Money generates money. Manufacturing is a combination of labour and financial aspects. A good combination of these aspects will yield better results. Accurate prediction may remove all hurdles to achieve the desired goals of the firm. The top-level management of the firm should take a good decision to provide better returns to the shareholders.

Important Aspects of Financial Management in Working Capital: The financial management is guardian to the shareholders. It always thinks about the welfare of shareholders in order to maximize their wealth. Wealth creation to the shareholders is one of the important aspects of the financial management. Financial manager is an administrator of financial resources. He has to take proper precautions about the functioning of the firm in all aspects. Finance spread every corner of the company. Financial manager should manage assets efficiently like fixed assets, tangible assets, moveable and immovable assets of the firm. He has to look after all aspects of the current assets and current liabilities. He has to select the best sources of finance to current assets and current liabilities. He has to take precautions regarding working capital management such as duration of time, proportion of working capital in total assets of the firm. He has to prepare good planning for smooth functioning of the production schedules. He must devote much time for internal management of the firm. It is necessary to manage working capital in the best possible way to get maximum benefit to the shareholders. The financial manager should also design the constituent of the current assets in total assets of the firm. He must decide the extent of working capital in the total assets of the firm. A small firm faces several problems in financing current assets. Generally, large organizations can raise financial resources very easily due to image of the firm. It is easy for raising for financial resources for higher goodwill of the company. High reputed firms can assess to capital market at any time to meet their financial needs. The finance manager should also have a vision about the growth of the firm.

Capitalisation: The term capitalization means the total amount of capital deployed in a business. It is an important and inner element in financial plan. It occupies a dominant role in making of a financial plan of the company. Plan is necessary in the business environment. A careful financial plan provides best results. The execution of financial plan is the testing factor for the top-level management. Capitalization is a part of financial plan. In other words, capitalization is an estimation of total amount of capital raised, types of different kinds of financial instruments, and deciding of capital mix. It is a quantitative and qualitative phenomenon of the capital. It explores the quality of capital introduced in a business environment. The quality of input may provide better–finished product from the organization. The quality of capital may be described as low cost of funds, at a right mix of blended capital and it is raising efficiency from the capital market. Different scholars in various ways have defined capitalization. The scholars of financial management are not unanimous in exploring the meaning of capitalization. As per the various definitions submitted by different scholars, we may conclude that capitalization is the sum of par value of stocks and bonds outstanding. Hence, capitalization means a combination of par value of share capital, debentures, and bonds. Some of the scholars do not take reserves and surplus as part of capitalization. In practice, every business enterprise utilizes the reserves and surplus of resources in the business. It is highly impossible to demark the capital, reserves, and surplus. Therefore the popular model of capitalization refers the deployment of financial resources as follows:

PAR VALUE OF SHARE CAPITAL+RESERVES AND SURPLUS + LONG TERM LOANS

Capitalization is more popular and widely used term in the corporate sector. It is not pronounced in case of sole trading and partnership firms. Capital means the net worth of a commercial enterprise. The assets minus liabilities are known as net worth. Promoters of the company will decide about the quantum of amount to be raised, type of securities to be issued by the company. However, determination of financial requirement and mobilization of resources is a highly intellectual and efficient task. The theory of capitalization depends upon two factors. (a) cost theory, (b) earning theory.

(a) *Cost Theory*: Cost theory is useful to the top-level management of the company. It is clearly indicates the quantum of amount to be raised from the capital market. It enables the management to take a decision to raise financial resources from the capital market. This theory has certain limitations. It does not define actual meaning of net worth of a commercial enterprise. According to this theory capitalization means, the cost of fixed assets, the amount of working capital, and the floating expenses of the business enterprise. The net worth of a business enterprise depends upon its earning capacity. This theory is not useful for the companies, which have irregular earnings. This theory ignores the importance of depreciation in valuation of assets of the organization.

(b) *Earning Thoery*: This theory is based on earning capacity of a business enterprise. It undertakes the true value of the company. In this method, the net worth of a company will be measured based on its earning capabilities. There is a correlation between capitalization and earning capacity of the firm. It clearly indicate the productivity of the capital deployed in the business. Newly established organizations should estimate their average annual earnings, taking into consideration of industry's capitalization rate. This theory is quite difficult to the new entrants because they are unable to predict accurate future earnings. It is very easy to compute their earnings for established companies. If the new company fails to assess the future earnings, the capitalization based on earnings might have proved more risky to the company. All consequences should be faced by the new organization. A new organization will have to face several problems in the business environment. Therefore, the newly established organizations should adopt the "cost theory" for selection of capitalization. Earnings theory is suitable for newly established organizations.

The capitalization of company may be arrived by adding the value of paid up share capital, reserves, surpluses, etc., this is known as actual capitalization. Capitalization of the corporate sector can be categorized into two kinds:

(a) Under-capitalization
(b) Over-capitalization

(a) *Under-capitalization*: Under-capitalization means the real value of assets is reflected more than the book value. It is an excess of true asset value over the aggregate of stocks and bonds outstanding. Under-capitalization can be described, as the real value of share is more than the book value of share. In this state, the company will generally have a high rate of earnings. Under-capitalization and inadequate capital is different from each other. Some people may create confusion about these two situations. If a company fails to pay its commitments is termed as inadequacy of capital. Under-capitalization does not mean for non-payment of its commitment. There is slight difference from inadequacy of capital to under-capitalization. Broadly, speaking, non-payment of its commitment is not the situation of under-capitalization in all aspects. Under-capitalization occur in the following situation:

(a) If the company fails to estimate about initial earnings.
(b) If the company fails to use high capitalization rate.
(c) High standard of efficiency.
(d) Economic situations.
(e) Dividend policy of the company.

Under-capitalization effects on the functioning of the corporate sector. It encourages high competition in the market. It provides higher wages to workers. It also provide high dividend to shareholders. It is useful to the management for manipulation of share prices in the stock market. Government will control theses organizations and get more taxes from them. Tax revenues are more important to the Central Government. The Central Government will be happy if the tax revenues are more. However, in the same context, we must remember that, consumers will be exploited. A high rate of goods will hurt the consumers and it is harmful to the society. Consumer and society always expect a low rate of goods at high quality durables.

Under-capitalization may be corrected by taking remedies by the company management. The management will take a decision to split the equity of the company. Splitting up of share will reduce dividend pressure on the profitability of the company. Issue of bonus shares is another appropriate remedial measure taken by the company management. This situation arise a reduction in dividend per share.

Under-capitalization is not more harmful to the society and company. It is an indication of financial strength. It is not an economic problem. It can be corrected more easily. Therefore, every company should have a proper capitalization.

Over-capitalization: Over-capitalization is an excess flow of capital in relation to its working capacity levels. It reflects lower profitability levels of the company. The earning capacity of the firm will reduce when the company reaches over-capitalization situation. The earning capacity may fall due to either internal or external problems. If the company earnings declined, the organization is not in a position to pay its expenses such as interest and dividend. Hence, the company fails to meets it promises made to the shareholders and debentureholders. The company will lose the confidence of the share and debentureholders. There is no scope for raising of resources from the capital market due to lost of investor's confidence. The earning capacity of the firm is not relatively to the extent levels of available financial resources. This is a situation of over-capitalization. Over-capitalization may also be noticed with the comparison of book value of share and real value of share. If the book value of share is more than real value is known as 'Over-capitalization'. Generally, the book value of the share can be ascertained through net assets available to equity shareholders as per book value of the company. Over-capitalization clearly indicates that, the available capital is not utilized properly. Capital is a scarce commodity. The company should utilize it in a proper way. It clearly indicates inefficiency of the company. A scarce commodity should be utilized with utmost satisfaction of the shareholders. Shareholders may not forgive for under utilization of financial resources. They loose the confidence about the functioning of the company. They will never support to the future expansion or diversification proposals made by the company. Hence, over-capitalization the company with high skills should carefully handle problem. It can be arise due to the following situations:

(a) If a company procures more money from the market than its actual requirements.
(b) If a company, pay more rate of interest towards financial cost.
(c) If a company make insufficient provision of depreciation and replacement cost.
(d) A higher rate of taxation may also cause this situation.
(e) It also arises due to higher expectation of earnings or lower rate of capitalization rate.
(f) If a company purchases assets with inflated cost.

Over-capitalization can be said that, excess capital is not used properly. However, there is a difference between over-capitalization and excess capital. Over-capitalization exists when the company's earnings declines substantially. Excess capital arises when the company procures more capital from the market than its necessity. Additional financial resources may not generate additional profits relatively. Hence, it may be noted that excess capital and over-capitalization is not the same situation. They are both different aspects.

However, over-capitalization and under-capitalization are harmful to the company and society. Both of these two aspects are bad, but over-capitalization are more harmful to the society and company. Therefore, the company should have a proper supervision about these aspects.

2

Investment Decision: Capital Budgeting

Introduction: The basic objective of the financial management is to look after the welfare of shareholders. The shareholders may be satisfied with two elements, dividend and capital appreciation. Dividend is a reward to the shareholder for his accepting level of risk. A business enterprise can satisfy the shareholders when it shows excellent performance in the business. Business is a game of return and risk. An intelligent business organization can reduce its risk levels and capture the profit. Profit is a jam and risk is ginger. Every human being always wants jam. No one is interested to invite risk. Risk can be escapable in some situations and not avoidable. Therefore, the management of a business enterprise depends upon several decisions. Decisions will definitely influence the profit levels. Investment decisions directly show an impact on the profitability of the organization. The day-to-day operations of the business enterprise requires several investment decisions. The correct decision of the investment may lead to grow the organization exponentially. Investment means contribution to various securities. It refers to invest funds in various securities like shares, bonds, debentures and other financial assets. It just like parking place of financial resources. The financial manager is concerned with the deployment of funds in various avenues of investments. He should take into consideration of the welfare of the shareholders of the company before making any investment decisions. He is related to financing and deployment of surplus resources for achieving the desired goal of the firm. Financing decision is the most important aspect in the financial management area. It is related to the long-term financial requirement of the company and the sources, which the fund is to be raised. It also searches about the low cost funds. Therefore, the financial manager must design the optimum capital structure. The financial manager should always think about the low cost funds and risk. He should determine the amount of long-term finance requirement of the firm keeping in view of the company's policies. He has to decide the asset composition of company. Generally assets are broadly classified into two kinds, (a) fixed assets, (b) current assets. The financing aspects of fixed assets is known as capital budgeting.

Meaning of Capital Budgeting: A good financial planning is useful to reach the companies desired goals. Capital budgeting means planning for capital assets. Capital assets are also known as fixed assets. The financing decision of the fixed assets is called capital budgeting. The capital budgeting decision is related to take an investment decision whether to invest or not to invest in a project. The projects may be either setting up of a factory or purchasing sophisticated machinery or creating additional capacities to produce more goods. The financial manager should analyze various alternatives regarding their profitability and risk associated with them. He should evaluate various alternatives available to him and choose best alternative model in order to fulfill the goals of the firm. He should also be taken into consideration of social responsibility of the business. Therefore, the capital budgeting decisions are important, crucial, and critical. It is a comparison process of cost against benefits over a long period. The investment decisions should consider several factors such as profitability, safety, liquidity, and solvency.

Capital budgeting is an important function of the financial manager. He should evaluate different alternatives and expose the information to the board members for making a good decision.

Importance of Capital Budgeting Decisions : Capital is a scared commodity. It is precious metal. It should be utilized in a proper way otherwise, the shareholders will burnt their money in the company. The capital budgeting decisions arises in the following situations:

(a) New technology
(b) Sales
(c) Diversification
(d) Inventions
(e) Legal formalities

(a) *New Technology*: Technology is an important factor in the digital era. It occupies a dominant role in the production function of area of management. In this modern world, the market is highly competitive, and the customer always demands high quality and low price. As per the requirement of customers, the corporate sector should produce goods as per the trend in the market. The demanding nature of high quality goods and at low price is forced the corporate sector to sell the goods at reduced price levels. Therefore, the corporate sector followed the cost reduction progammes in order to meet the requirement of modern customers. The management of the corporate sector taken a decision to reduce the cost of production with latest technology. Technology is the most important tool in manufacturing process. It occupies a dominant role to reduce the production cost substantially. New technology enables the corporate sector to produce the goods at lower cost and with high quality of goods. It also enables the corporate sector to gain substantial savings in the form of time saving. Time is another important and influential factor in selection of best technology. The latest technology produces more goods in short period of time rather than traditional methods. The corporate sector noticed the importance of new technology and they adopted that by paying heavy amount of fees or royalty. For adopting new technology, it requires a capital budgeting decision. The series of consequences should be taken into consideration by making capital budgeting decisions. The replacement of existing machinery and importing of latest machinery and technology needs the deployment of heavy funds in the business. Hence the importance of capital budgeting arises in this situation.

(b) *Sales*: A high quality product enjoys good sales in the market. It will became market leader and enjoys the brand image. A good brand image and goodwill of the company will definitely boost the sales of the organization. Increased sales of goods may lead to the expansion of the business. An expansion of the business requires capital budgeting decision. Hence, the company should make investment decision regarding capital expenditure of additional plant capacity. The financial manager should estimate the financial requirement of the company when the company goes in expansion. He should take all precautions about the series of events occurring during the expansion process. It requires high efficiency to handle this situation.

(c) *Diversification:* Diversification is the important aspect in the life of the corporate sector. Risk is always follows the profit. A business organization can reduce its risk by entering into another field of operations of the business. It requires an additional amount of capital expenditure for purchase of new machinery and other establishment expenditure. The finance manager should draw the project planning and be able to execute the things as per schedule. Excellence in execution enables us to grow better than competition, produce at lower costs, meet customer expectations, and become consistently successful. Achieving superior performance is the key to competitive advantage. A speedy execution is the mother of good fortune. The financial manager should assess the cost of delay in project execution. A delay in execution is a costly affair. The delay in execution of project implementation in Air India and Indian Airlines has lost their market dominance. A delay in the National highway corridor plan conceived by the government at a cost of Rs.11, 000 crores have been ended with Rs. 30, 000 crores. Another example, the Bangalore International Airport has escalated the cost from Rs. 2000 crores to Rs. 6000 crores. In the private sector, there are other examples where one witnessed the fruits of execution excellence. Reliance Industries Jam Nagar refinery was completed in 24 months, making it a record of sorts in the petrochemical industry world-wide. It turned out to be a giant masterstroke that helped the company grow leaps and bounds in revenues and profits and emerge eventually as an undisputable leader in the private sector.

(d) *Inventions:* Research is the most important factor in the manufacturing process. Continuous research activities may leads to upgrade the present technology. An investment in upgrading technology is more useful to the corporate sector on long-term basis. Hence, the finance manager should take a good decision to allocate the funds towards R&D sector. A large amount of funds require to establish laboratory and sponsoring the research project.

Legal Formalities: All business organizations are rotating according to the Government policies. Government policies always influence the business environment. If the government issues a notification for installation of pollution, equipments in the factories require a higher amount of funds. Therefore, the corporate sector needs to implement the legal formalities of the government as per the latest provisions and legislature in order to satisfy the rules and regulations.

Capital budgeting is a long-term planning for proposed capital outlays and the mode of financing. It requires a careful execution of the projects and is helpful to achieve the desired goals. The capital budgeting decisions can be classified as follows:

(a) Mutually exclusive decisions.
(b) Accept reject decisions.
(c) Contingent decisions.

Mutually exclusive decision means, analysis of two or more business opportunities or alternative available to the company. A careful analysis of different alternatives provides various proposals. It indicates whether a project may be taken up or not to be taken by the company.

Accept or reject decisions means, exposing the information when the projects are independent and do not compete with each other. The financial manager will transmit the information whether to accept or reject the project based on minimum return on the required investment. He should make a comparison and select the best alternative, which provides more than desired return.

Contingent decisions are dependable proposals. The decision in investment in one project requires another additional capital outlays. *For example* if a company selected a project to establish a project in backward area needs to make additional investment capital outlays in roads, building of houses, hospitals, schools, etc.

Rationale of Capital Expenditure: Capital expenditure means investment of funds in new machinery and projects. The financial manager should be cautious about risk involved in new projects. He must be able to see the introduced capital must be utilized efficiently. Efficient utilization of funds is the basic objective of the financial management. Generally, all business organizations have to continuously invest in business for replacement of machinery or expansion or improving its efficiency. The firm's basic objective is to maximize the return and minimize losses. This objective can be achieved by either increasing operational profit or cost reduction. Hence, the capital expenditure may be occurred in two situations: (a) increase of profit related to expenses, (b) introduction of cost reduction process. Capital expenditure increases the revenues of the firm by expanding its activities. If the company replaces the old machinery and old technology, will definitely reduces cost of production by introducing new technology and new machinery.

Capital investment decisions are more important in the corporate sector. The decisions may increase the profitability and achieve its desired goals. If firm works efficiently, it can achieve its desired goals or otherwise there will be a chance to attack by risk. Risk is always a haunting factor behind profit. It may not be think that an increase in capital expenditure some times could not generate sufficient profits. Hence, by injecting an additional capital into the business may or may not be generate adequate profits. However, the following factors will influence the capital investment decisions.

(a) Size of Fund
(b) Return on Investment
(c) Targeted Profit
(d) Priority of Projects.
(e) Risk

(a) *Size of Fund:* Fund is a scared commodity. It should be utilized for achieving its desired goal of the firm. If a firm has vast financial resources, it can take a decision without verifying any other factors. It can accept all projects, which generate more profits. It will rationalize the decisions when funds are limited. Hence, the firm will make a decision according to the available financial resources only. The finance could be able to draw financial requirement of the company based on outflow and inflow of the cash. It is better to analyze the consequences of the inflow and outflow of cash during expansion or diversification stage. The financial manager should carefully take a decision on the following aspects:

(a) New project cost
(b) Preliminary expenses
(c) Working capital

The financial manager should prepare the financial requirement of new project. Investment in new project may lead to introduction of additional capital. He should take a decision, by undertaking a new project should not be disturb existing project. He should take all precautions that a new project cannot reduce the working capital of the company. He should adjust the amount of sale of the old assets to the new project. The financial manager of the company should also make tax adjustment on sale of the assets. He should also be required to assess the tax liability on the transactions occurred on sale of assets. He should also consider various investment allowances available under the tax provisions.

(b) *Return on Investment:* The fundamental principle of financial management is to earn a minimum rate of return on every financial commitment of the firm. He will be responsible for monitoring of the funds. The fund should earn minimum return based on its cost of capital. The cost of capital is most influencing and important factor in determining the capital expenditure decisions. *For example* if a firm raises financial resources at a cost of 12 per cent, the company will not like to accept the proposal, which yields a rate of return less than 12 per cent. The projects giving a yield below the desired rate of return will be rejected. Therefore, the financial manager should keep in mind about cut off rate of the investment.

(c) *Targeted Profit*: Capital investment decisions are more important in commercial enterprises. The decision should increase revenues of the business enterprises. The financial manager should assess the future earnings of the company. The decision contains two elements, accounting profit, and cash flows. Accounting profit is an income concept related to accounting process. In accounting process, gross revenue will be treated as cash flows. The cash flows of the business enterprise will not subtract depreciation charges and other amortization expenses. The cash flow approach is based on the following aspects. Economic utility, accounting process, time factor. Economic value of the project is the basic factor in determining capital expenditure decisions. It is associated with cash inflows and outflows of the project. The financial manager will make a comparison that, the initial investment may warrant to its cash inflows during lifetime of the project. Accounting profit is a controversial method to some extent. The ambiguities will arise due to different accounting policies and practices regarding assessment of inventory, depreciation, expenses, etc. Hence, the account of profit may show differently due to different account policies and procedures followed by the business organizations.

Time is one of the most important and influencing factor in case of new projects. Generally, profit is a paper figure. Not all payments may be settled at once. Therefore, the time taken in realizing or making payments is completely ignored. The cash flow approach undertakes the importance of the time factor while making capital expenditure decisions.

(d) *Priority of Projects*: Financial manager is concerned with the evaluation of different alternative projects, before company management. He will play an important role when a company searching for a better project to make investment decision. If a number of projects available to the company on an acceptable rate of profit, it should rank the projects according to their profitability. The company should rank all the projects according to their earning capabilities. The ranking of projects leads to arise when the capital is scarce. The objective of ranking is to look after the better utilization of monetary resources.

(e) *Risk*: Risk is a general phenomenon in every business sector. It may be escapable and unavoidable. It is a fundamental principle that high return ventures attracts high risk, low return ventures create low risk. Therefore, different investment proposals have different degrees of risk and uncertainty. Risk may be defined as "the chance of future loss that can be foreseen." Risk comprises all elements, which cause for the variability in the return. It may be arise by the factors such as wrong selection of investment, wrong timings, maturity, etc. It also may arise due to general economic conditions, competition, technological developments, consumer tastes, and preferences, labour problems. The risk can be divided into the following major types: *Default Risk, Financial Risk, Business Risk, Liquidity Risk, Maturity Risk, Call Risk, Interest Rate Risk, Inflation Risk, and Currency Risk.*

Importance of Capital Budgeting: Capital expenditure decisions will occupy an important role in the life of the business enterprise. It is the most crucial and critical business decision. The top-level management of the company should take a special care before making investment decisions. The following factors may influence the capital investment decisions.

(a) Large financial resources.
(b) Long period.
(c) Logical decisions.

Capital expenditure decisions needs large amount of financial resources. It is not an easy task to raise finance from the capital market or other sources. The company should make a proper plan for the fulfillment of heavy investment programme. At the same time, it should be observed that any wrong decision of investment decision might jeopardize the organization.

Capital expenditure decisions are involved to invest the money in long-term projects. Therefore, the entire investment made by the company will not be recouped in a short period. Hence, the company management shall wait to get the fruits of its investment results on long-term period. The deployment of heavy fund in business may not generate profits immediately.

Capital expenditure decisions are based on logic. The company keeping in view of its earning capabilities will take the decisions. If a company takes a decision, it may not irreversible. Therefore, the company should think twice before making final investment decision.

Capital expenditure decisions are related to top-level management of the company. It includes both planning for proposed capital outlays and their financing. Investment opportunities may be identified or created. At present, the market is having full of competition and it is not easy to sell the product to the customers. In order to attract the customer, every company is going to influence the customer by offering goods at competitive prices. Competitive prices tend the companies to reduce the selling prices drastically. Hence the corporate sector always try to incorporate cost reduction programmes. Cost reduction programmes include replacement of old machinery, improving the efficiency of installed capacity, adopting new technology methods, improving the manufacturing process, at plant levels. Sometimes the company may also add a new product to its portfolio due to demand from customers. The investment proposals may arise at different levels within a firm. Most of the investment idea generate from the plant level. In India, more than 50 per cent of investment proposals from the corporate sector generates from plant levels. Marketing department of the company may also occupy a key position to take investment proposals. Idea generation is the most important factor in investment decision of various proposals. The corporate management of the Indian companies provides freedom to its human resources to expose new and innovative products to fulfill the needs of the modern Indian customer. The corporate sector generally adopts three methods for introduction of new products. (a) Research studies, (b) suggestions from employees, (c) advices from consulting firms. Research is the highly influential and important factor in discovery of a new product or services. Research means searching for new methods, new process, and new technology. Technology is the dominant factor in the development of a nation. A sophisticated latest technology enhances the efficiency levels of the productivity. Improving the productivity levels stimulates the profitability of the corporate sector. Indian companies generally allow their employees to provide suggestions in finding of new investment proposals. The employees are encouraged to offer their suggestions to expose new initiatives. The companies will generally give top priorities where the suggestions came from workers. The important factor to get advices from consulting firms. Consultancy services are available in the market for new products. Goldman Sach, ABC consultants, Itcot, KPMG, ORG, MARG, IMRB, etc. are the best examples for providing the services required by the corporate sector. Therefore, the decision of capital investment lies with the top-level management of the company. The management should spend its time to make an investment decision and for its follow up and execution of the new project. Capital budgeting decision lies with top-level management and it involves three levels. A. Operating B.Administrative C. Strategic. Operating capital budget level is related with routine expenditure such as office automation. Junior level management may easily handle the office automation. Administrative capital budgeting handles the expansion programmes of the company. Expansion is the most important factor in the corporate sector to accumulate profits continuously. A strong sales turnover in the market, brand loyalty in the market, tends to go for expansion. Brand image stimulates the profitability of the company. Goodwill of the company will definitely useful to take investment decisions by the middle management. Middle management of the company is responsible for making capital budgeting decisions to medium range investments. Strategy is one of the important factors related to top-level management of the company. Strategic capital budgeting involves in acquisition of new units by the company. It requires a careful and financial analysis of the series of consequences. Acquisition is the turning point to a commercial enterprise. It is an indication of stability in the business environment, which the company rotates. Strategy is a long-term planning of the company. Strategic planning is a top down process.

CAPITAL BUDGETING APPRAISAL METHODS

Capital budgeting is related to provision of funds for specified investment decisions of the company. It undertakes all the aspects of financial consequences of the investment decisions. The top-level management will make project appraisal and evaluation before making a decision. There are several methods and techniques for evaluating different projects. The financial manager of the concern is to compare, different proposals advantages and disadvantages in order to fulfill the desired goals of the firm. The capital budgeting appraisal methods are presented below:

1. Payback method.
2. Discounted cash flow method.
3. Accounting rate of return.

1. *Payback Method*: Payback method is one of the methods in appraisal of capital budgeting techniques. It is oldest and commonly used method. It deals with the recoupment of investment made by a company in the business. It requires recovering its investment within a stipulated period. It represents the period in which the total investment in permanent assets payback itself. In this method time factor will play a major role in taking decisions. The business concern wants to its investment to recover as early as possible from its business operations. It gives top priority to the projects, which generates more cash inflows within short period. It selects the projects where the shorter period recovery is possible. The longer period project may reject and shorter period will be selected in this method. It analyses different alternatives available, compares all aspects, and make an investment decision for quick recovery of its capital

invested in a project. In case of evaluation of a single project, it will be selected within period as desired by the board of directors. The top-level management will set broad guidelines for taking up a new investment proposals as a policy matter. If the project is unable to recover its investment within period, the company may not select the project. It gives priority to higher cash inflows and shorter time of recovery of investment. The business is involved with risk and uncertainty. The commercial enterprise always thinks about its safety of the principal at first and profit is next. Profit is an important factor for any kind of commercial enterprise, but safety of capital occupies a dominant role in making of investment decisions. However, profit is an inner element of the corporate sector but liquid is also important and influencing factor for making of investment decisions. It contains two elements, annual cash inflows, and initial investment. In business, environment cash inflows are most important factor. Sales occupy a dominant role in the cash inflow. Sales are the most important and dominating factor in all aspects of the corporate sector. A strong sales turnover will keep the company in a pleasant manner and it enhances the managerial capabilities. Initial investment is an important factor in the life of a business enterprise. The large and reputed organizations were built up with a low amount of capital in the history. Infosys was established with an initial investment of Rs. 25,000. The company approached various banks for a loan of Rs. 2,00,000 at the initial period. Therefore, a small investment will give a path to bigger opportunities. The appraisal method of the project should distinguish between acceptable and non-acceptable. It should be a convenient method to choose among several alternatives. The payback method fulfills desired goals of a business enterprise where they give top priority for shorter period projects. This method gives priority for bigger profits and quick recovery of investment as early as possible. The payback method has its advantages and disadvantages. The advantages are presented below:

(A) Payback method is useful in high uncertainty, political instability, and rapid technological environment. It is a simple method to understand. It is useful to the newly established companies towards payment of dividend to shareholders, because after recovery of its initial investment, the firm will start paying rewards to owners. The disadvantages of the system will be as follows:

(a) The payback method ignores the firm after recovery of its investment from the project.
(b) Long gestation period projects may not be taken up by this system.
(c) It ignores the financial cost of the firm.

The payback method is suitable for projects less than 3 years. If a project, exceeding three years period seems to be quite hazy. It provides liquidity to the firm. It gives priority to liquidity rather than profitability. Liquidity is an important aspect in financial management. Therefore, some firms give top priority to the liquidity, then this method is more suitable for such type of organizations. It is suitable for short-term performance showing organizations.

2. *Discounted Cash Flow Method*: Discounted cash flow method give importance to profitability and time. This method is becoming popular day-by-day. It is an improvement of payback method. It gives priority to get the return after payback period. It depends upon cash inflow and outflow. It considers profit after tax only. It will be calculated with the help of discount factors. It recognizes that rupee of today is worth more than rupee one received at a future date. It will compare the cash inflows and outflows. This method can be classified as follows:

(a) The Net Present Value Method.
(b) Present Value Index Method.
(c) Internal Rate of Return.

(a) *The Net Present Value Method*: The net present value method takes into consideration of the time value of money. It is a modern method of evaluating investment proposal. It gives priority for rupee received today. It undertakes into consideration of cash inflows during the life period of the project. It calculates each year cash inflows and outflows with discount factor. It will compare with the pre-determined rate of return framed by the management. This rate is known as "cut-off rate." The top-level management of the company will frame cut-off rate based on cost of capital. The cost of capital is a highly influencing factor in financial aspects of the corporate sector. Finance is a scarce commodity. It is precious. Its availability depends upon many factors. The fund is the important factor for all decisions of the business enterprise. It is available in the market at fluctuating interest rates. The financial resources may be raised by the corporate sector in a good economic environment. The capital market is helpful to the corporate sector for raising of financial resources. The goodwill of the company is necessary to raise the resources from the market. This method will take into consideration of cash inflow and outflow. Cash inflow represent in the form of profit after tax. It includes depreciation. Cash outflow consists investments made by the firm in different stages in various projects. The working capital of the firm will be a part of cash outflow of the starting year. According to this method, a project will be accepted, if it is positive. The positive factor will be observed when the present value of cash inflows is more than present value of cash outflows. The dominant position of the cash inflows influences to take an investment decision. If the project generates negative results, it will be rejected. The dominant position of present value of cash outflow tends the company, not to accept the proposal. Therefore this method suggest whether a project can be undertaken or not with the help of discount factors and a combination cash flows.

(b) *Present Value Index Method:* Present value index method provides a comparison of different investment proposals. It is a refinement of the net present value method. It can be computed by comparing the total of present value of future cash inflows and the total of the present value of future cash outflows. The present value index method will be reflected in the form of percentage. It is known as benefit cost ratio. The high percentage of present value index project may be selected.

(c) *Internal Rate of Return*: Internal rate of return is another method of computation of investment evaluation proposal. This method undertakes the consideration of time value of money. It considers all the cash inflows generated by the project during the life period of the asset. Internal rate of return is that rate at which the sum totals of cash inflows after discounting equals to the discounted cash outflows. The internal rate of return is the discount rate, which makes net present value of the project equal to zero. The internal rate of return represents rate of return on the uncovered investment balance in the project. It is also known as time adjusted rate of return. It was popularly known as trial and error method. This method selects a project, which provides a higher rate of return. It is useful for comparison of different project proposals. The calculation of internal rate of return is a laborious process. It will be arrived after many calculations. It is not easy to understand.

3. *Accounting Rate of Return Method*: Accounting rate of return method is known as average rate of return. It undertakes the importance of profitability of a project. The profitability of the project will be computed as per the accepted accounting principles. It undertakes the entire economic life of the project. This method will be calculated based on average yield. According to this method, the project will be accepted, if it generates more return than the expected rate of return of the company. Any project, which generate below the rate of return of the company's will be rejected. A series of number of project will be evaluated by this method and a decision will be taken, where the projects generate more than expected rate of return of the company. Accounting rate of return method is not popular in these days. This method does not take into account the time value of money. The accounting rate of return will be calculated in different ways. Each method provides different results. The reliability of this method is quite doubtful.

PRACTICAL PROBLEMS IN CAPITAL BUDGETING

Illustration No. 1

Gowthami Industries Ltd. provides the following information. It manufactures goods by manual labour and is examining the proposals to introduce latest machinery. In the market, three alternative models are available. Prepare a statement of profitability showing the payback period method. As a financial manager of the company, how you are going to analyze the situation to the top-level management of the company.

Particulars	*Machine A*	*Machine B*	*Machine C*
Life of the machine	5yrs	6yrs	7yrs
Savings in scrap	1000	1500	2000
Savings in wages	7000	8000	9000
Additional maintenance cost	1200	1400	1600
Additional supervision	1600	1800	2000
Cost of machine	12000	20000	30000

There are no corporate taxes.

Solution:

Statement Showing Annual Cash Inflows of Machines

Particulars	*Machine A*	*Machine B*	*Machine C*
Life of the machine	5yrs	6yrs	7yrs
Savings in scrap	1000	1500	2000
Savings in wages	7000	8000	9000
Total savings	8000	9500	11000
Additional cost of maintenance	1200	1400	3000
Additional cost of operation	800	3100	2000
Total addl. cost	2000	4500	5000
Net Cash Inflow	6000	5000	6000

Payback period for machine a = original investment/average annual cash inflow

Payback period for machine a = 12000/6000 = 2 years
Payback period for machine b = 20000/5000 = 4 years
Payback period for machine c = 30000/6000 = 5 years

Machine A has shorter payback period. This machine recovers its investment very quickly in 2 years. Therefore machine A is better to select for buying.

Illustration No. 2

L&T is an engineering company. The company intends to purchase a new machine for its factory purpose. In the market, four alternative models are available. You are required to examine the various alternative models and suggest to the management for buying of new machine from the market.

Particulars	*Machine M*	*Machine N*	*Machine O*	*Machine P*
Investment	4,00,000	5,00,000	6,00,000	7,00,000
Sales	6,00,000	7,00,000	8,00,000	8,50,000
Production expenses				
Raw Material	80,000	90,000	95,000	95,000
Wages	70,000	50,000	55,000	60,000
Factory	75,000	65,000	60,000	70,000

Particulars	*Machine M*	*Machine N*	*Machine O*	*Machine P*
Administrative cost	30,000	25,000	40,000	50,000
Selling and distribution expenses	15,000	20,000	25,000	30,000
Scrap value	40,000	40,000	30,000	80,000
Life of Machine	3 yrs.	4 yrs.	3 yrs.	5 yrs.
Interest on capital	8 per cent per annum			
Income tax	50 per cent			

Solution:

Statement Showing the Net Cash Inflow of Four Machines

Particulars	*Machine M*	*Machine N*	*Machine O*	*Machine P*
Total cost (2)	2,70, 000	2,50,000	2,75,000	3,05,000
Investment	4,00,000	5,00,000	6,00,000	7,00,000
Sales (1)	6,00,000	7,00,000	8,00,000	8,50,000
Depreciation(4)	1,20,000	1,15,000	1,90,000	1,24,000
Interest on capital (5)	32,000	40,000	48,000	56,000
Life of the machine	3 yrs	4 yrs	3 yrs	5 yrs
Profit before depreciation and interest.(1-2=3)	3,30,000	4,50,000	5,25,000	5,45,000
Depreciation and interest(4+5=6)	1,52,000	1,55,000	2,38,000	1,80,000
Profit before tax (3-6=7)	1,78,000	2,95,000	2,87,000	3,65,000
Income tax 50 per cent	89,000	1,47,500	1,43,500	1,82,500
Profit after Tax	89,000	1,47,500	1,43,500	1,82,500
Add; depreciation	1,20,000	1,15,000	1,90,000	1,24,000
Net cash inflow	2,09,000	2,62,500	3,33,500	3,06,500
Payback period	1.91 yrs	1.94 yrs	1.79 yrs	2.28 yrs.

INVESTMENT/NET CASH INFLOW

Recommendation: From the above analysis, it is better to select machine 'O' because it recovers the investment very quickly.

Note: The total cost is a combination of raw material, labour, factory overheads, administrative cost, selling and distribution cost.

Illustration No. 3.

The following information is available from the finance department of a commercial organization. You are required to select best project from the available data according to payback method.

Particulars	*Project-A*	*Project-B*	*Project-C*	*Project-D*	*Project-E*
Investment	8,00,000	9,00,000	7,00,000	6,00,000	5,00,000
Profit	2,00,000	2,50,000	1,50,000	1,75,000	2,50,000
Depreciation	10%	10%	10%	10%	10%
Income tax	50%	50%	50%	50%	50%

The depreciation of the project should be charged on straight-line method.

Solution:

Statement Showing Annual Cash Inflow of Projects

P/s	*Project-A*	*Project-B*	*Project-C*	*Project-D*	*Project-E*
PBT	2,00,000	2,50,000	1,50,000	1,75,000	2,50,000
(-) Tax	1,00,000	1,25,000	75,000	87,500	1, 25,000
PAT	1,00,000	1,25,000	75,000	87,500	1, 25,000
(+) Depr.	80,000	90,000	70,000	60,000	50,000
Total	1,80,000	2,15,000	1,45,000	1,47,500	1,75,000
Cash inflow					
Investment	8,00,000	9,00,000	7,00,000	6,00,000	5,00,000
PAY	4.44yrs	4.18yrs	4.82yrs	4.06yrs	2.85yrs

BACK PERIOD

The above analysis shows that the project E should be selected because it provides immediate cash inflow of the investment. It recovers in shorter period of 2.85 years. (Corrected)

Illustration No. 4

From the following particulars compute (a) payback period (b) post-payback profitability (c) post back profitability index.

P/S investment annual cash inflow estimated life period scrap value.

Project super	75,000	15,000	12 years	0
Project supreme	75,000	20,000	12 years	0
Project deluxe	75,000	18,000	10 years	0

Solution:

Computation of Payback Period of Different Projects

Payback period	=	Investment/annual cash inflow
For project super	=	75,000/15,000 = 5 years
For project supreme	=	75,000/20,000 = 3.75 years
For project deluxe	=	75,000/18,000 = 4.16 years.
Post-payback profitability	=	Annual cash inflow (estimated life-payback period)
For project super	=	15,000 (12-5)
		15,000 (7) = 1.05,000
For project supreme	=	20,000 (12-3.75)
		20,000 (8.25)
		1,65,000
For project deluxe	=	18,000 (10-4.16)
		18,000 (5.84)
		1, 05,120

Post-payback profitability index for project super 1,05,000/ 75,000 x 100=140%

For project supreme 1, 65,000/75,000 x 100 = 220%.

For project deluxe 1, 05,120/75,000 x 100 = 140.16%

Illustration No. 5

From the following information calculate payback period, post-payback profitability, post payback profitability index of different projects.

P/S	*Project-A*	*Project-B*	*Project-C*	*Project-D*	*Project-E*	*Project-F*
Investment	60, 000	60,000	60,000	60,000	60,000	60,000
Cash inflows						
1st year	10,000	12,000	15,000	20,000	6,000	3,000
2nd year	10,000	12,000	15,000	20,000	6,000	3,000
3rd year	10,000	12,000	15,000	20,000	6,000	3,000
4th year	10,000	12,000	15,000	20,000	6,000	3,000
5th year	10,000	12,000	15,000	20,000	6,000	3,000
6th year	5,000	6,000	7,500	10,000	10,000	15,000
7th year	5,000	6,000	7,500	10,000	10,000	15,000
8th year	5,000	6,000	7,500	10,000	10,000	15,000
Life	8 years	8 years	8 years	8 years	8 years	8 years

Solution:

Calculation of Payback Period of Different Projects

Payback period=Investment/annual cash flows

For project A = 60,000
10,000+10,000+10,000+10,000+10,000+5,000+5,000 = 7 years

For project B = 60,000 12,000+12,000+12,000+ 12,000+12,000=5years

For project C = 60,000 15,000+15,000+15,000+15,000 = 4 years

For project D = 60,000 20,000+20,000+20,000 = 3 years

For project E = 60,000
6,000 + 6,000+6,000+6,000+6,000+10,000+10,000+10,000= 8yrs

For project F = 60,000
3,000+3,000 +3,000+3,000+3,000+15,000+15,000+15,000 = 8yrs

Calculation of post-payback profitability = Annual cash inflows × rest of payback period

For project- A = 5000 x 1= 5000
For project- B = 6,000 x 3 = 18,000
For project- C = 37,500
For project- D = 70,000
For project- E = 0
For project- F = 0

Post-Payback Profitability Index for Project A=

Post-Pay-back Profitability × 100/Investment

Project A	=	5000 x 100/60,000	=	8.33%
Project B	=	18,000 x 100/60,000	=	30%
Project C	=	37,500 x 100/60,000	=	32.5%
Project D	=	70,000 x 100/60,000	=	11, 66%
Project E	=	0 x 100/60,000	=	0
Project F	=	0 x 100/60,000	=	0

Illustratiion No. 6

The following information is available to you. You are required to calculate discounted payback period of the project.

Investment of the project Rs. 1, 50,000, life of the project 6 years, annual cash inflow of the project Rs. 50,000, discount factor 10 per cent.

Solution:

Calculation of Present Value of Cash Inflows

Year	Inflow	PV Factor at 10 per cent	Present Value	Cumulative Present Value
1.	50,000	.909	45,450	45,450
2.	50,000	.826	41,300	86,750
3.	50,000	.751	37,750	1,24,300
4.	50,000	.683	34,150	1,58,450
5.	50,000	.621	31,050	1,89,500
6.	50,000	.564	28,200	2,17,700

The cumulative present value of cash inflows at the end of 3rd year is 1, 24,300 and it is at the end of 4th year is 1, 58,450.

Hence, the payback period may be in between 3 and 4 years. It may be calculated as follows:

Discounted payback period = 3 years+25,700/34150=3.75 years

Illustration No. 7

From the following information, rank the projects as per payback period method.

Particulars	*Investment*	*Annual cash inflows*	*Estimated life of the project*
Project M	1,00,000	25,000	6 years
Project N	80,000	16,000	7 years
Project O	40,000	8,000	8 years
Project P	1,50,000	30,000	7 years
Project Q	2,00,000	80,000	5 years
Project R	1,20,000	40,000	4 years
Project S	1,80,000	45,000	6 years
Project T	2,10,000	70,000	5 years
Project U	1,80,000	90,000	3 years

Solution:

Ranking of the Projects According to Payback Period

Project	*Investment*	*Annual cash inflow*	*Payback period*	*Rank*
Project M	1,00,000	25,000	4 Years	4th
Project N	80,000	16,000	5 Years	5th
Project O	40,000	8,000	5 Years	5th

Project P	1,50,000	30,000	5 Years	5th
Project Q	2,00,000	80,000	2.5 Years	2nd
Project R	1,20,000	40,000	5 Years	5th
Project S	1,80,000	45,000	4 Years	4th
Project T	2,10.000	70,000	3 Years	3rd
Project U	1,80,000	90,000	2 Years	1st

Illustration No. 8

Harish Industries Limited present the following information The Company examine two alternatives. Calculate (a) return on investment, (b) payback period, (c) discounted payback period, (d) profitability index. The present value of Re. 1 to be received at the end of each year, at 10 per cent p.a. is given below:

Year	*1*	*2*	*3*	*4*	*5*
p.v.	*.91*	*.83*	*.75*	*.68*	*.62*

Particulars	*Project A*	*Project B*
Investment	1,00,000	1,40,000
Life of the project	5 years	5 years
Net income (after depreciation and tax)		
End of 2000	2,500	—
End of 2001	10,000	17,000
End of 2002	17,500	17,000
End of 2003	12,500	17,000
End of 2004	—	17,000

The project requires an additional amount of working capital of Rs. 10,000. The additional amount will be earned by the project after the expiry of the project. The company adopted straightline method of depreciation.

Solution: The project generates cash inflows for five years. The depreciation for project A is calculated as follows:

Depreciation for project A = investment/life of the asset = 1,00,000/5=20,000

Depreciation for project B = investment/life of the asset = 1,40,000/5=28,000

There is no scrap value for the projects.

CALCULATION OF PROFIT AFTER TAX

Year	Project A			Project B		
	Net Deprcn.	Cash Inflow	Income	Net Deprcn.	Cash Inflow	Income
2000	2,500	20,000	22,500	—	28,000	28,000
2001	10,000	20,000	30,000	17,000	28,000	45,000
2002	17,500	20,000	37,500	17,000	28,000	45,000
2003	12,500	20,000	32,500	17,000	28,000	45,000
2004	—	—	—	17,000	28.000	45,000
Total	42,500	80,000	1, 22,500	68,000	1, 40,000	2.08.000

(a) Return on Investment

Calculation of ROI for project A = Average investment/average return × 100

Average investment of project A = total net income/no. of years.

Average return on average investment = average investment/ average return × 100

Calculation of return on investment of the Project A and Project B

Particulars	Project A	Project-B
Investment	1,10,000	1,50,000
Life	5 years	5 years
Total net income	42,500	68,000

Average investment for project A = 42,500/4 = 10,625
Average investment for project B = 68,000/4 = 17,000
Average return for project A = 11000+10,000
= 1, 20,000/2 = 60,000
Average return for project B = 1, 50,000+10,000
= 1, 60,000/2 = 80,000
Average return on average = 10,625/60,000 x
investment for project A 100 = 17.70%
Average return on average
investment for project b = 17,000/68,000 x 100=25%.

(b) Calculation of Payback Period for Project A

Year	Cash in Flow
2000	22,500
2001	30,000
2002	37,500
2003	10,000
	1, 00,000

Average cash inflow 1,00,000/4 = 25,000
Payback period 1,10,000/25,000 = 4.4 years

Calculation of Payback Period for Project B

Year	*Cash Inflow*	
2000	28,000	
2001	45,000	
2002	45,000	
2003	22.000	
	....	Payback period is 3.48 Yrs
	1,40,000	
	....	

(C) Discounted Payback Period Method

Year	*PV Factor*	*Project A* Cash Inflow	PV of Cf	*Project B* Cash Inflow	PV of Cf
2000	.91	22,500	20,475	28,000	25,480
2001	.83	30,000	24,900	45,000	37,350
2002	.75	37,500	28,125	45,000	33,750
2003	.68	32,500	22,100	45,000	30,600
2004	.62	—	—	45,000	27,900
Total PV			95,600		1, 55,080
Less; investment			80,000		1, 40,000
			15,600		15,080

Discounted Payback

Year	*Project A* *PV of Cash Inflows*	*Project B* *PV of Cash Inflows*
2000	20.475	25,480
2001	24,900	37,350
2002	28,125	33,750
2003	22,100	30,600
2004	—	27,900

Payback period for Project A 6500/22,100=.29
Payback period for Project B 12820/27,900=.46

Therefore, Project A payback period is 3.29 years and Project B is 3.46 years.

(d) Profitability Index Method

For project a = 15,600/80,000 x 100 = 19.5%
For project b = 15080/1, 40, 00 x 100 = 10.77%

DISCOUNTED CASH FLOW TECHNIQUE

Illustration No. 9

Hindusthan Engineering Company Limited is thinking about to purchase of a new machine. The company is considering two alternative models, which are available in the market. Two alternative machines X and Y have been suggested. The machines involve an investment of Rs. 6,00,000 and requiring Rs. 30,000 as additional working capital at the end of the 1st year. The earnings after taxation are expected to be as follows:

Year	Cash Inflows	
	Machine X	Machine Y
1	60,000	1.80,000
2	1, 80,000	2, 40,000
3	2, 40,000	3, 00,000
4	3, 60.000	1, 80,000
5	2, 40,000	3, 60,000

The company requires a return on capital of 10 per cent. You are required to compare the profitability of machines and state which alternative you consider financially preferable.

The present value of Re. 1 due in a number of years

Year	1	2	3	4	5
Pave at 10%	0.91	0.83	0.75	0.68	0.62

Solution:

Hindusthan Engineering Company Ltd. Statement Showing the Profitability of the two Machines as per NPV Method

Machine B is preferable. The cash inflow of machine B is higher than machine A. Machine B generates more cash inflows. Hence, it is suggested that the company should go for selection of project B as per capital budgeting technique.

Year	Discount	Machine-A Cash Inflow	Present Value	Machine-B Cash Inflow	Present Value
1.	0.91	60,000	54,600	1, 80,000	1, 63,800
2.	0.83	1,80,000	1,49,400	2, 40,000	1, 99,200
3.	0.75	2,40,000	1,80,000	3, 00,000	2, 25,000
4.	0.68	3,60,000	2,44,800	1, 80,000	1, 22,400
5.	0.62	2,40,000	1,48,800	3, 60,000	2, 23,200
Total Present Value of Cash Inflows			7, 77,600		9, 33,600
Total Present Value of Cash Outflows			6, 27,300		6, 27,300
Net Present Value			50,300		3, 06,300

Illustration No. 10

Gowthami traders is planning to install either of the two machines, which are mutually exclusive. The particulars of the following information reveal financial aspects. The machine A will recover salvage value of Rs. 3, 000 and machine B will recover Rs. 2, 000 in the 6th year. The cost of capital is 10 per cent; the two machines will operate the same efficiency. Determine which machine is cheaper?

Year		Machine A	Machine B
Investment cost	0	20,000	16,000
Operating cost	1	4,000	5,000
	, 2	4,000	5,000
	, 3	4,000	5,000
	, 4	5,000	7,500
	, 5	5,000	7,500
	, 6	5,000	7,500
	, 7	6,000	
	, 8	6,000	
	, 9	6,000	
	, 10	6,000	

Present value of 10%		year 1-	.9091	year-2	8264
year 3-	.7513	year 4-	.6830	year-5	6209
year 6-	.5645	year 7-	.5132	year-8	4665
year 9-	.4241	year 10-	.3855		

Present value of an annuity of Re. one per period at 10 per cent discounting factor.

At the end of year 6 = 4.3553 at the end of year 10 = 6.1446

Capital recovery factor at 10 per cent for 6 years =.2296 for 10 years =.1628

Solution:

Statement Showing the Computation of Equivanlent Annual Cost of two Machines

Year	Machine A	P.V.Factor 10 Per cent	Discounted
0	Cost 20,000	1.0000	20,000
1	4,000	.9091	3,636
2	4,000	.8264	3,305
3	4,000	.7513	3,005
4	5,000	.6830	3,415
5	5,000	.6209	3,104
6	5,000	.5645	2,822
7	6,000	.5132	3,079
8	6,000	.4665	2,799
9	6,000	.4241	2,544
10	6,000	.3885	2,331
			50,040

Cost after accounting for salvage value:

50,040-3000 x .3885 = 50,040- 1165=48,875

Equivalent annual cost = total discounted cost x capital recovery cost

50,040 x.1628 = 8146.51

Year	Machine b	PV Factor 10 Per cent	Discounted cf
0	16,000	1.0000	16,000
1	5,000	0.9091	4,545
2	5,000	0.8264	4,132
3	5,000	0.7513	3,756
4	7,500	0.6830	5,122
5	7,500	0.6209	4,656
6.	7,500	0.5645	4,233
			42,444

Cost after accounting salvage value: 42,444-2000 x .5646
42,444-1129 = 41315

Equivalent annual cost = 42,444 × .2296 = 9745. Hence machine A is cheaper.

Illustration No. 11

Harish Engineering Company is planning to make an investment decision regarding two alternative machines available in the market. From the following information, calculate the net present value of the two projects and suggest which of the following should be accepted at a discounted rate of 10 per cent.

Particulars	*Project-M*	*Project-N*
Initial investment	40,000	60,000
Life of the asset	5 years	5 years
Scrap value	2,000	4,000

The profit before depreciation and after taxes (cash flows) is as follows:

Year	*Project M*	*Project N*
Ist Year	10,000	40,000
IInd Year	20,000	20,000
IIIrd Year	20,000	10,000
IVth Year	6,000	6,000
Vth Year	4,000	4,000

Solution:

Calculation of Present Value of Project M

Year	*Cash Inflows*	*PV at 10 Per cent*	*PV of Net Cash Flows*
1.	10,000	.9091	9091-00
2.	20,000	.826	16,520-00
3.	20,000	.751	15,020-00
4.	6,000	.683	4,098-00
5.	4,000	.621	3,726-00
5.	2,000	.621	1,242-00
			49,697-00

Present value of all cash inflows	49,697 - 00
Less present value of initial investment	40,000 - 00

Net present value	9,697 - 00

Calculation of Present Value of Project N

Year	*Cash Inflows*	*PV Factor*	*Present Value of Net Cash*
1.	40,000-00	.909	36,360-00
2.	20,000-00	.826	16,520-00
3.	10,000-00	.751	7510-00
4.	6,000-00	.683	4,098-00
5.	4,000-00	.621	2,484-00
5.	Scrap 4, 000-00	.621	2,484-00

Total Present Value of Inflows			69,456-00

Less: Present Value of Initial Investment	60,000-00
Net Present Value	9456-00

The net present value of project M is higher than project N. Hence, the project M should be accepted as per the NPV approach.

Illustration No. 12

A limited company is planning to make an investment decision for a project. It requires a capital outlay of Rs. 4,00,000. The following information is related to the proposed project. The annual income after depreciation but before tax is as follows:

Year	*Rs.*
1.	2,00,000
2.	2,00,000
3.	1,60,000
4.	1,60,000
5.	80,000

Depreciation may be taken as 20 per cent on original cost and taxation at 50 per cent of net income

You are required to evaluate the project as per net present value method. The discounted factor is 10 per cent.

Solution:

Statement of Net Cash Inflow

Year	Profit after Deprecn.	Income Tax	Profit Before Depreciation after Tax
1.	2,00,000	1,00,000	1,80,000
2.	2,00,000	1,00,000	1,80,000
3.	1,60,000	80,000	1,60,000
4.	1,60,000	80,000	1,60,000
5.	80,000	40,000	1,20,000

Calculation of Discounted Cash Flows

Year	Net Profit Before Deprcn but after Tax	PV 10 per cent	Present Value
1.	1, 80,000	0.909	1,63,620-00
2.	1, 80,000	0.826	1,48,680-00
3.	1, 60,000	0.751	1,20,160-00
4.	1, 60,000	0.683	1, 09,280-00
5.	1, 20,000	0.621	74,520-00

PV of Cash Inflows			6,16,260-00
Less; Initial Investment			4,00,000-00

			2.16,260-00

Illustration No. 13

Vani Textiles are considering two mutually exclusive projects. These projects require an initial investment of Rs. 1, 00,000 each and have a life of five years. The cost of capital is 10 per cent and income tax rate is 50 per cent. The company charges depreciation on straitline method. The estimated net cash inflows before depreciation and tax of the two projects as follows:

	Project X	*Project Y*
1.	40,000	60,000
2.	44,000	54,000
3.	56,000	44,000
4.	50,000	50,000
5.	60,000	40,000

Which project should be selected as per net present value method?

Solution:

Calculation of Cash Inflows of Project-X

Year	Cash inflow before Deprcn. in Addition, Tax.	Depre-ciation	Profit after Depre-ciation	Income Tax	Profit after Depre-ciation and Tax	Profit before Depre-ciation and after Tax	Discount Factor @ 10%	Present value of Cash Inflows
1	2	3	4	5	6	7	8	9
1	40,000	20,000	20,000	10,000	10,000	30,000	0.91	27,300
2	44,000	20,000	24,000	12,000	12,000	32,000	0.83	26,560
3	56,000	20,000	36,000	18,000	18,000	38,000	0.75	28,500
4	50,000	20,000	30,000	15,000	15,000	35,000	0.67	23,800
5	60,000	20,000	40,000	20,000	20,000	40,000	0.62	24,800

Total Present Value of Cash Inflows;	1, 30,960
Less: Initial investment	1, 00,000
Net Present Value	30,960

Calculation of Cash Inflows of Project–Y

Year	Cash inflow before Deprcn. in addition, tax.	Depre-ciation	Profit after Depre-ciation	Income Tax	Profit after Depre-ciation and Tax	Profit before Depre-ciation and after Tax	Discount Factor @ 10%	Present value of Cash Inflows
1	2	3	4	5	6	7	8	9
1	60,000	20,000	40,000	20,000	20,000	40,000	0.91	36,400
2	54,000	20,000	34,000	17,000	17,000	37,000	0.83	30,710
3	44,000	20,000	24,000	12,000	12,000	32,000	0.75	24,000
4	50,000	20,000	30,000	15,000	15,000	35,000	0.68	23,800
5	40,000	20,000	20,000	10,000	10,000	30,000	0.62	18,600
								1,33,510

Total Net Present Value of Cash Inflows;	1,33,510-00
Less: Initial Investment	1,00,000-00
Net Present Value	33,510-00

From the above analysis, it is better to select project Y because it provides more present value of amount.

Illustration No. 14

Gowthami Engineering Company is thinking about to buy a machine, brand A for the manufacture of a new product at an investment of Rs. 2, 00,000.

The annual operating costs are estimated at Rs. 75,000 excluding depreciation and these costs are estimated based on an annual production of 1, 50,000 units of production. The fixed costs at this volume of production are an amount of Rs. 7, 50,000 per annum. The selling price is Rs. 6 per unit of out-put. The machine has a five-year life and it provides no scrap value.

The company has now searching for another alternative model "DELUX". The model is capable of giving the same volume of production at estimated annual operating costs of Rs. 40,000 exclusive of depreciation. The fixed costs will however remain the same in value. This machine also will have a five-year life without scrap value. The investment of the machine is Rs.1,75,000.

The management of the company has an offer for the sale of the brand A at Rs. 75,000 and the cost of removal thereof will amount to Rs. 15,000. Please ignore income tax.

Therefore, the company management found that the operating costs are low. In view of the lower operating costs, the company intends to dismantle the brand A model. It further thinks that for installation about deluxe brand. It is observed that the model A has not yet started commercial production and that the time lag in the removal thereof. The project cost of capital is found 14 per cent and the present value factors for five years are 0.88, 0.80, 0.68, 0.60, and 0.52.

As a financial manager of the company, state whether the company may replace model A machine by buying super model machine and provide your suggestion.

Solution:

Statement Showing Computation of Net Present Value of Super Model Machine

CASH OUTFLOW OF SUPER MODEL MACHINE

Investment of the machine 1, 75,000-00
Less: Sale of brand A model of machine (75,000-15,000)
60,000 -00

(a) Net cash outflow on deluxe model 1, 15,000 -00
Incremental cash inflow from deluxe brand
Annual cash inflow from deluxe 1, 33,750
Annual cash inflow from brand A 75,000
Net incremental cash inflow 58,750

(b) Present value of incremental cash inflows for five years at 14 per cent 58,750 x 3.43 = 2, 01,512.50

(c) Net present value of deluxe brand model 2,01,512-1,15, 00=86,512=00

Therefore the net Present Value is Positive

Independent Evaluation of Model A and Delux Model

Particulars	*Brand A*	*Deluxe Model*
Cash outflow (Invest.)	2,00,000-00	1,75,000-00
Less: Present value of cash Inflows for five years at 14% Brand A 75,000 (.88+.77+.66+.60+.52 =3.43 75,000 x 3.43=	2, 57,250	
Less: Pvcf	2, 57,250-00	3, 08,750-00
	------------------	------------------
	57,250=00	1, 33,750

Inflows for five years at 14%. 3.43 x 90,000 1, 33,750-00

Computation of Cash Inflows of the two Models

Particulars	*Brand A*	*Delux Model*
Annual production	1, 50,000	1, 50, 000
Selling price per unit	Rs. 6	Rs, 6
Sales	9,00,000	9, 00,000
Less: Operating costs	75,000	40,000
	------------	------------
	8, 25,000	8, 60,000
Less: Fixed cost	7, 50,000	7, 50,000
	------------	------------
Annual cash inflow	75,000	90,000
	------------	------------

Therefore it is Better to Buy Delux Model of the Machine.

Illustration No. 15

Harish Engineering Limited is specialized in electronic goods. They have recently developed technology to design a new product. They are quite confident of selling this product. They intended to produce 10,000 units. The investment for this project is Rs. 30,00,000. The project will have an economic life of four years and no significant terminal salvage value. In the first four years, the promotional expenses are planned as follows:

Year	*Advertisement*	*Other Expenses*
1.	1,05,000	60,000
2.	85,000	80,000
3.	75,000	90,000
4.	45,000	1,20,000

The company incurred additional fixed operating cost for this new product is estimated at Rs. 75, 000 per year. The company requires 15 per cent of profit after taxes on its investment. The corporate tax is on an average works to be 50 per cent. The company follows depreciation of straight-line method. The variable cost of producing and selling the unit would Rs. 300 per unit. The present value of annuity of Rs. One received or paid in a steady stream for four years at 15 per cent is 3.0079. From the information available, you are required work out a selling price per unit of the product keeping in view with the company-required rate of return.

Solution: The company intends to produce a new product. The production of new product will be undertaken keeping in view of financial goal of the firm. Therefore, let us first calculate the annual cash outflow of the organization. The second step requires computing the net present value of cash inflows as per the financial values.

ANNUAL CASH OUTFLOW

Particulars	*Rs.*	
Total variable cost per year 10,000 x 300		30,00,000
Promotional expenditure per year	1, 65,000	
Fixed operating costs per year	75,000	
	-------------	2, 40,000

	32,40,000
Less: income tax at 50%:	16,20,000

	16,20,000
Tax advantage on depreciation	3,75,000
30, 00,000 x 1/4 x 50/100 = 3, 75,000	--------------
	12,45,000

PRESENT VALUE OF CASH OUTFLOW

Present Value Factor for Four Years @ 15% 3.0079

12, 45,000 x 3.0079 =	38,33,355
Add: Initial investment	30,00,000
Present value of cash outflow	68,33,355

Tax implications: The total cash outflow of the project Rs. 68, 33,355 is divided by 3.0079. Rs. 22, 71,802

Therefore the required annual revenue before tax 22, 71,802 x 100/50=45,43,604

Hence the selling price per unit = 45,43,604/10,000=454

Illustration No. 16

Gowthami Industries Ltd., intends to undertake a product in their factory. The following financial information is available to you: As a financial manager of the company, you are required to draw conclusions about the plans. A product is currently manufactured on a plant. The plant was bought for Rs.1,50,000 six years ago. The plant is not depreciated fully for tax purpose and it has a book value of Rs. 70,000. The cost of the product is as follows:

Particulars	*Unit Cost*
Direct material	28.00
Indirect labour	10.00
Other variable overheads.	18.00
Fixed overheads	20.00

	76.00

The company produces 12,000 units per annum. It intends to use the old machine in future and spending an amount of Rs. 50,000 towards repairs.

The company is searching for another with suitable new machine that should be in latest technology. The latest equipment is available with an investment of Rs. 4,00,000. The old machine will be trade off for Rs. 55,000. The projected cost of the product will be as follows:

Particulars	*Per Unit Rs.*
Direct cost	18.00
Indirect labour	14.00
Other variable overheads	14.00
Fixed overheads	22.00
	68.00

The fixed overheads of the plant and machinery will be allocated from other departments including depreciation.

The company sold the old machine in the open market for Rs. 50,000. The new machine will have a life of 10 years and the scrap value is Rs. 25,000. The income tax rate of the corporate sector is 50 per cent. The company-required rate of return on investment is 10 per cent. The company charges depreciation on new and old machinery for 10 years. The company assumes the future sales will be stable. Ignore capital gains tax. As a financial manager of the company, please provide your suggestion regarding buying of new machine. The present values of ten years as follows: 0.91, 83 0.75, 0.68, 0.62, 0.56, 0.51, 0.47, 0.42 and 0.39 respectively. In addition, present value of annuity of Re. 1 for 10 years at 10 per cent discount rate is 6.1446:

Solution: The data will be processed for arriving at accurate conclusion for buying a new machine by the company. The analysis will be done in four steps. In the first step, it requires the calculation of annual depreciation for new machine, in the second step old machine depreciation will be computed. In the third step computation of two machines annual cash outflows will be done. In the fourth step, the incremental effect will be studied.

Step 1. Computation of Annual Depreciation on New Machine

Particulars	*Rs.*
Investment of the machine	4,00,000-00
Add: Sale proceeds of the old plant	55,000-00

Total cost of the new machine	4,55,000-00
Less: Salvage value	25,000-00

	4, 30,000-00

Annual Depreciation on New Machine
4, 30,000 x 10/100=43,000

Second Step calculation of annual depreciation on old machine.
Book value of old plant is 70,000

Therefore, the Depreciation of Old Machine is Rs. 7,000

Step 3. Computation of Net Cash Outflows of the two Machines

Particulars	*Old Machine*	*New Machine*
Production of units per annum	12,000	12,000
Variable cost per unit	56	46
Cash outflow due to total variable Cost of the project.	6, 72,000	5, 52,000
Repairs per annum	50,000	—
Fixed overheads for depreciation	7,000	43,000
	------------	------------
	7, 29,000	5, 95,000
Less: Income-tax savings	3, 64,500	2, 97.500
	------------	------------
	3, 64,500	2.97,500
Less: Non-cash outflows *i.e.* deprcn.	7,000	43,000
	------------	------------
	3, 57,500	2, 54,500
	------------	------------
Add: Savings in annual cash outflows due to purchase of new machine	—	1, 03,000
	------------	------------
	3, 57,500	3, 57,500
	------------	------------

Step 4. Computation of Net Present Value of Savings, if New Machine is Purchased

Particulars	*Rs.*
Annual savings in cash outflows for life of the asset	1,03,000
Present value of total savings in cash inflows for ten years	------------
1, 03,000 x 6.1446	6,32,894
Add: Present value of cash inflow at the end of 10th year	
on account of salvage value 25,000 x 0.386	9,650

	6,42,544
Less : Present value of cash outlay in the initial year	4,00,000

Net present value of saving	2,42,544

Therefore, the above financial analysis reveals that the purchase of new machinery provides positive results. Hence the proposal may be accepted and it found financial viable. The company can arrange for deploying the new machine.

Illustration No. 17

Jyothy Engineering Limited is considering the purchase of new machinery. There are two alternative models available in the market. They are X and Y. They are involved with a cost of Rs. 1,25,000. The expected cash flows from the two machines are presented below. As a financial consultant, which project would you propose to select the new machine?

Year	*Cash Inflow Investment A*	*Investment B*
1.	*Rs.*50, 000	*Rs.*60, 000
2.	45,000	50,000
3.	35,000	40,000
4.	30,000	40,000

The company has a financial goal to earn 10 per cent on investment. The risk premium rates are 2 per cent and 8 per cent respectively for investment A and B.

Solution: The financial consultant shall examine various aspects in buying of a new machine. At the first instance, he should compare the profitability of the two investments based on net present value of cash inflows adjusted for risk premium.

Computation of Present Values of Cash Inflows of the two Projects

Year	Investment A Discount Factor	Cash Inflow	pvcf at 12%	Investment B Discount Factor	Cash Inflow	pvcf at 18%
1.	0.89	50,000	44,500	0.847	60,000	50,820
2.	0.80	45,000	36,000	0.717	50,000	35,850
3.	0.71	35,000	24,850	0.609	40,000	24,360
4.	0.64	30,000	19,200	0.516	40,000	20,640
			1, 24,550			1, 31,670

The net present value of the two investments;
Project A 1,25,000- 1,24,550 = -450
Project B 1,25,000- 1,31,670 = 6,670

Hence, the project B can be considered. Project A provides negative returns and project B yield positive return of Rs. 6,670.

Illustration No. 18

Bhageeratha Engineering Company is searching for a better good project. It provides financial data for two projects. As a financial manager of the firm, you are required to suggest the firm which project is more beneficial to the firm.

The Investment of these two Projects requires Rs. 35,000 each.

Year	Project A		Project B	
	Cash Inflow	Co-efficient	Cash Inflow	Co-efficient
1.	30,000	0.7	25,000	0.8
2.	25,000	0.6	35,000	0.7
3.	25,000	0.9	25,000	0.6

The company is willing to take a decision for deployment of funds in a financially viable project. The risk free cut off rate is 10 per cent.

Solution: From the above financial information, it requires computations in two steps. In first instance, it needs to compute cash inflows with certainty. In second step, the cash inflows arrived from step 1 will be multiplied with discount factors of the cut off rate of the project.

Computation of Cash Inflows with Certainty

Year	Project A			Project B		
	Cash Inflow	Co-efficient	pvcf	Cash Inflow	Co-efficient	pvcf
1.	30,000	0.7	21,000	25,000	0.8	20,000
2.	25,000	0.6	15,000	35,000	0.7	24,500
3.	25,000	0.9	22,500	25,000	0.6	15,000

Computation of Present Values of Cash Inflows

Year	Discount Factor @ 10 Per cent	Project A		Project B	
		Cash Inflows	Present Values	Cash Inflows	Present Values
1.	0.90	21,000	18,900	20,000	18,000
2.	0.83	15,000	12,450	24,500	20,335
3.	0.75	22,500	16,875	15,000	11,250
			48,225		49,585

Net present value from project A = 48,225–35,000 = 13,225
Net present value from project B = 49,585–35,000 = 14,585

From the above financial information, it is better to select project B. It generates more cash inflows than project A.

Illustration No. 19

Rajesh Engineering Limited is interested to know the more risky project from the available information. As a financial consultant, which project would you suggest? The degree of risk may be based on standard deviation.

Project A		Project B	
Cash Inflow	Probability	Cash Inflow	Probability
3,000	0.3	3,000	0.2
5,000	0.3	5,000	0.3
7,000	0, 2	7,000	0.3
9,000	0.2	9,000	0.2

Solution: The financial data will be processed further to know more risky project. It requires two steps. The first step involves computation of standard deviation of the both projects.

Calculation of Standard Deviation of Project A

Cash Inflows	*Deviation from Mean 6000*	*Square of Deviations*	*Probability*	*Weighted Square root of Deviations*
1	*2*	*3*	*4*	*5*
3,000	-3000	90, 00,000	0.3	27, 00,000
5,000	-1000	10, 00,000	0.3	3, 00,000
7,000	+1000	10, 00,000	0.2	2, 00,000
9,000	+3000	90, 00,000	0.2	18, 00,000
Standard Deviation of the Project A =				50, 00,000

Square root of 50,00,000/1 = 2236.06

Calculation of Standard Deviation of Project B

1	*2*	*3*	*4*	*5*
3,000	-3000	90, 00,000	0.2	18, 00,000
5,000	-1000	10, 00,000	0.3	3, 00,000
7,000	+1000	10, 00,000	0.3	3, 00,000
9,000	+3000	90, 00,000	0.2	18, 00,000
				42, 00,000

Square root of 42, 00,000/1= 2049.30

Therefore, the data explores the riskiness of the two projects. Project A is more risky than project B. Hence the company should select project B because of it provides less risk.

Illustration. No. 20

Mahesh Engineering Limited has the following investment opportunities. As a financial consultant, which proposal would you select from various alternatives?

Proposals	*Initial Investment*	*Profitability Index*
1.	2, 50,000	1.12
2.	1, 75,000	1.10
3.	2, 25,000	1.09
4	2, 00,000	0.07

The company has a surplus amount of funds is available for Rs. 3, 50,000.

Solution: The company is searching for better investment alternative. Therefore, it should be analyzed based on net present value of investment. The net present value of proposal 1 may be found as follows:

2, 50,000 x (1.12-1) = 2, 50,000 x 0.12=Rs.30,000

Net present value of proposal 2 and 3 is presented below:

Proposal 2 1,75,000 x (1.10-1.00) = 1, 75,000 x 0.10 = 17,500

Proposal 3 2,25,000 x (1.09-1.00) = 2, 25,000 x 0.09 = 20,250

37,750

The above numerical information reveals that the proposals 2 and 3 provide more benefits, whereas proposal 1 generates Rs. 30,000 only.

INTERNAL RATE OF RETURN

Illustration No. 21

Kasturi Industries Limited are interested to select a project. As a financial consultant of the company, you are requested to analyze two alternatives and select best one as per the principles of internal rate of return method.

Particulars	*Project X*	*Project Y*
Investment	15,000	14,000
Cash inflows		
Year 1	7,000	2,000
Year 2	3,000	2,000
Year 3	2,000	3,000
Year 4	6,000	11,000

Solution: From the above analysis, it is observed that the cash inflows are not uniform. Therefore, internal rate of return will have to be calculated by the trial and error method. In this analysis at the first step factor should be found. The factor indicates the relationship between investment and cash inflows. The factor can be computed by the following formula:

F = I/C
Factor = Factor to be located
I = Original investment
C = Average cash inflows per year
The factor in case of project X would be = F= I/C
Investment = 15,000
C = Average annual cash inflows
7,000+3,000+2,000+6,000=18,000/4=4,500
Therefore F = 15,000/4,500=3.33
The factor in case of project Y would be as follows:
F = I/C
I = Initial Investment
C = Average annual cash inflows =
2,000+2,000+3,000+11000=18,000/4=4,500
F = 14000/4,500=3.11
The factor found in case of project X = 3.33
The factor found in case of project Y= 3.11

The factor should be verified in table of present value of Re. 1 received annually for N years. The arrived digits should be verified on the line representing number of years corresponding to estimated useful life of the asset. Therefore the project X will have a useful life period of 4 years. The factor should be verified in line of 4 years in the said table.

In case of project, it was found that 3.33 are available in the table at 8 per cent column. Hence, it should be calculated at 8 per cent and the result should be shown equal to investment amount. Otherwise, it should be calculated repeatedly unto tallying of investment amount of the project.

Calculation of Present Value of Cash Inflows of Project X

Year	*Cash Inflows*	*Discounting Factor at 8 per cent*	*Present Value of Cash Inflows*
1	7,000	0.93	6510
2	3,000	0.86	2580
3	2,000	0.79	1580
4	6,000	0.73	4380
			15,050

Therefore, the project X internal rate of return is 8 per cent. In the similar way project Y factor was found as 3.11. It should be verified in the table on similar lines of 4 years of useful life period of the project. It was found as 12 per cent. Therefore, the present value should be calculated as follows:

Year	Cash Inflows	Discounting Factor at 12 per cent	Present Value of Cash Inflows
1.	2,000	0.89	1780-00
2.	2,000	0.79	1580-00
3.	3,000	0.71	2130-00
4.	11,000	0.64	7040-00
			12,530-00

Therefore, the present value of cash inflows is less than the investment amount of the project at 12 per cent. Hence, the arrived 12 per cent is not correct and let us choose another rate in order to meet the investment amount of the project of Rs. 14,000. Let us assume as 10 per cent as project cost.

Year	*Cash Inflows*	*Discounting Factor at 10 per cent*	*Present Value of Cash Inflows*
1.	2,000	0.91	1820-00
2.	2,000	0.83	1660-00
3.	3,000	0.75	2250-00
4.	11,000	0.68	7480-00
			13,210-00

The present value of cash inflows at 10 per cent is less than the investment amount of the project. Hence, again let us select another rate in order to attain the investment amount of the project Rs.14,000. It should be 8 per cent. The following table will reveal the status of the project:

Year	*Cash Inflows*	*Discounting Factor at 8 per cent*	*Present Value of Cash Inflows*
1.	2,000	0.93	1860-00
2.	2,000	0.86	1720-00
3.	3,000	0.79	2370-00
4.	11,000	0.73	8030-00
			13,980-00

Therefore, the present value of cash inflows of the project is 13,980 which nearly 14,000 of the investment amount of the project. Hence, the internal rate of return is 8 per cent.

Illustration No. 22

Srinath traders are searching for a best machinery to install in their factory. The machine is intended to produce a luxury article, which commands demand for five years only. The initial investment of the project is Rs. 2,90,000 and its working capital is Rs. 20,000. The working capital amount will be realized at the of the end year of the project. The scrap value is expected at the end of the project life period is Rs. 6000 only. The earnings particulars of the company are as follows:

Year	*Earnings (Before Depreciation and Tax)*	*Tax Payable*
1.	95,000	25,000
2.	1, 35,000	35,000
3.	1, 75,000	45,000
4.	1, 20,000	20,000
5.	70,000	5,000

The present value factors at various rates of interest are given below. As a financial consultant, you are required to analyze the present value of cash inflows at various interest rates levels. Please indicate the internal rate of return of the project.

8%	10%	12%	14%	15%
0.93	0.91	0.89	0.88	0.87
0.86	0.83	0.80	0.77	0.76
0.79	0.75	0.71	0.67	0.66
0.73	0.68	0.63	0.59	0.57
0.68	0.62	0.57	0.52	0.50

Solution: The calculation of internal rate of return involves two steps. In the first step, cash inflows should be adjusted as per the tax adjustments. The next step is to calculate present values of the cash inflows at various levels of interest rates. The earning can be modified as follows:

95,000-25,000	=	70,000
1,35,000-35,000	=	1,00,000
1,75,000-45,000	=	1,30,000
1,20,000-20,000	=	1,00,000
70,000-5,000	=	65,000

Statement Showing Present Values of Cash Inflows

Year	Cash Inflows	8%	10%	12%	14%	15%
1.	70,000	65,100	63,700	62,300	61,600	60,900
2.	1.00,000	86,000	83,000	80,000	77,000	76,000
3.	1,30,000	1,02,700	97,500	92,300	87,100	85,800
4.	1,00,000	73,000	68,000	63,000	59,000	57,000
5.	65,000	44,200	40,300	37,050	33,800	32,500
		3,71,000	3,52,500	3,34,650	3,18,500	3,12,200

At 15 per cent of interest rate, the project generates Rs.3, 12,200 of cash inflows where the investment is equal; therefore, the internal rate of return of the project is 15 per cent.

Illustration No. 23

Janaki Industries Limited have an investment opportunity involving an amount of Rs. 50, 000. The project generates the following estimated net cash flow after taxes and before depreciation.

Year	Cash Inflow
1	8000
2	8000
3	8000
4	8000
5	8000
6	9000
7	11000
8	16000
9	11000
10	5000

Calculate the internal rate of return of the project using 10 per cent and 15 per cent of discount factor.

Solution:

Calculation of Internal Rate of Return of the Project at 10 per cent and 15 per cent Discount Factor

Year	Cash Inflow	10% Factor	Present Value	15% Factor	Present Value
(1)	(2)	(3)	(2 x 3) = (4)	(5)	(2 x 5)= (6)
1.	8,000	0.91	7280	0.87	6960
2.	8,000	0.83	6640	0.76	6080
3.	8,000	0.75	6000	0.66	5280

(1)	*(2)*	*(3)*	*(2 x 3) = (4)*	*(5)*	*(2 x 5)= (6)*
4.	8,000	0.68	5440	0.57	4560
5.	8,000	0.62	4960	0.50	4000
6.	9,000	0.56	5040	0.43	3870
7.	11,000	0.51	5610	0.38	4180
8.	16,000	0.47	7520	0.33	5280
9.	11,000	0.42	4620	0.28	3080
10.	5,000	0.39	1950	0.25	1250

Net present value at 10% =50,000-55060=5060
Net present value at 15%=50,000-44,540= (-5460)

Therefore, the present value at 15 per cent provides negative results and 10 per cent generates positive returns. Therefore, the internal rate of return will be calculated as follows:

The IRR of the project lies between 10 per cent and 15 per cent. Hence, the accurate internal rate of return can be computed as follows:

$$\frac{\text{10 per cent + positive npv @10 per cent}}{\text{Pv 10 percentage} - \text{pv 15 percentage}} \times (15\% - 10\%)$$

$$= \frac{10\% + 5060}{55060-44540} \times 5\%$$

$$= \frac{10\% + 5060}{10{,}520} \times 5\%$$

$$= 10\% + .481 \times 5\%$$

$$= 10\% + 2.4\% = 12.4\%$$

Hence, the internal rate of return of the project is 12.4 per cent.

Illustration No. 24

RAJ Industries Ltd. is searching for a project, which will yield the following returns over a period:

Year	*Cash Inflows*
1	85,000
2	85,000
3	95,000
4	95,000
5	80,000

The investment of the machinery involves Rs. 2, 25,000 and the asset is to be depreciated at 20 per cent per annum on written down value. Income tax rate is 50 per cent. The scrap value is zero. The cost of capital is 12 per cent. As a financial manager of the company, draw your conclusions and how will you explain to the top-level management regarding undertaking of this project. The present value of the rupee at the rate of interest is as follows:

Year	*1*	*2*	*3*	*4*	5
At 10%	0.91	0.83	0.75	0.68	0.62
At 14%	0.88	0.77	0.67	0.59	0.52

Solution:

Calculation of Internal Rate of Return

Year	*Yield*	*Deprcn.*	*Net yield*	*Tax*	*Net Cash PV*	*10%*	*PV Inflow*	*Pv 14 %*	*PV*
1	*2*	*3*	*4*	*5*	*(3+5) =6*	*7*	*8*	*9*	*10*
1	85,000	45,000	40,000	20,000	65,000	.91	59,150	0.88	57,200
2	85,000	35,500	49,500	24,750	60,250	.83	50,007	0.77	46,393
3	95,000	28,900	66,100	33,050	61,950	.75	46,462	0.67	41,506
4	95,000	23,200	71,800	35,900	59,100	.68	40,188	0.59	34,869
5	80,000	92,400	(12,400)	(6200)	86,200	.62	53,444	0.52	44,824
	4, 40,000		2,25,000		3, 32,500		2,49,251		2,24,792

Note One: The scrap value of the asset is zero. Therefore, the last year entire amount is treated as depreciation.

The investment is Rs. 2,25,000. The table reveals that the investment will earn 14 per cent of internal rate of return.

Illustration No. 25

ABC Industries Limited involved in manufacturing goods on a machine that is not fully depreciated for income tax purpose. The firm has current book value of Rs. 1, 50,000. The following financial information is presented for further analysis.

The variable cost per unit is Rs. 108:00 + fixed overheads Rs. 37 = 145=00

In the previous year the company produced 22,000 units and the firm paid expenses on repairs are expected to average Rs. 13,000 per month, the repairs cost is not included in the above financial information.

The company made an arrangement with the supplier of the machine as trade in for new equipment. The new machine would cost Rs. 9, 00,000 before allowing Rs. 2, 50,000 for the old equipment. The projected costs associated with the new machine are as follows:

The variable costs per unit is Rs. 87.00 + fixed overhead 43 = 130.

The fixed overheads are allocated from other departments and the depreciation of the equipment. The old machine can be sold at Rs. 1, 25,000 in the market. The new machine has an expected life of 10 years and Rs. 45,000 salvage at that time.

The income tax is 50 per cent. The cost of the new machine and book value of the old machine may be depreciated in 10 years. The rate is 14 per cent.

The demand forecasting of the product is 25,000 units. As a finance expert, you are required to give a suggestion for making investment decision. The present value of annuity of Re. 1 for 9 years @ 12% = 5.328. Present value of Re. 1 at the end of 10th year @ 12%= 0.319.

Solution:

Calculation of net present values of cash inflows accrued from the machine.

		Rs.
(i)	Net cash outflow for new machine	
	Investment of the machine	9, 00,000
	Trade in value of old machine	1, 25,000
	(a)	7, 75, 000

(ii) (a) Annual depreciation for new machine (Straight-line method)

$$\frac{9,00,000-45,000}{10}=85,500$$

(b) Annual depreciation for old machine 1,50,000/ 10,000 = 15,000

(iii)	Differential depreciation	
	Depreciation per annum for new machine	85,500
	Depreciation per annum for old machine	15,000
	(b)	70,500
	Differential depreciation extra for new machine	70,500

(iv) Cash savings from operations per year
If new machine is acquired
Variable cost of production 87 x 22,000 = 19,14,000-00

Variable cost of production in case of old machine is used

108 x 22,000 =	23,76,000
Repairs of old machine (13,000 x 12)	1,56,000

Old machine cost of operation	25,32,000

Therefore the differential cash savings on buying
6, 18,000
Per annum © ------------

(v) Differential cash flows after tax per annum
Because of new machine buying
For first nine years

Differential cash savings from operations (c)	6,18,000
Less: Differential depreciation (b)	70,500

Taxable savings	5,47, 500
Less: Tax at 55%	3,01,125

Net savings after tax	2,46,375
Add: Differential depreciation	70,500

Annual cash inflow after tax	3,16,875*

For 10th year

After tax cash inflow	3,16,875
Add: Scrap value of the new machine	45,000

	3,61,875

(vi) As per the financial numerical information, the old machine can presently be sold for Rs.1,25,000. Therefore, the company will loose the opportunity if the company retains the old machine or decides to replace it. Hence Rs. 25,000 financial resources are available under both alternatives.

Computation of Net Present Value (NPV)

Particulars	*Rs.*
The present value of cash inflows for 9 years at 12 per cent	
3,16,875 x 5.328	16,88,310
Cash inflow accruing at the end of 10th year	
3,61,875 x 0.319	1,15,438
Present value of total cash inflows	-------------
	18,03,748
Less: Present value of cash outflows	7,75,000

NPV	10,28,748

The financial information reveals that the net present value of project is Rs. 10,28,748 and therefore it is better to select new machine and replace old machine.

Illustration No. 26

XYZ company is a newly floated company. It is setting up a project with an investment of Rs. 3.50 crores. The company is examining to decide the location of the project. The Government of India rules indicates that a plant, which is located in backward area, provides a cash subsidy of Rs. 15,00,000. The rules further inform that tax concession is available for 10 years with 20 per cent exemption. Therefore, the company is thinking about location of the project in either forward area or backward area. The company is going to mobilize financial resources from the market. It borrows the fund at 12 per cent rate of interest from the lenders in forward area market. It has the capacity to borrow the funds from backward area at the rate of 10 per cent interest cost. However, as per the other analysis, the backward area involves higher revenue costs. The borrowed fund should be refunded in four equal annual installments. The first installment of the borrowed capital starts from the 4th year of commencement of project. The company adopts straight-line method of depreciation. From these particulars, as a financial consultant, you are required to draw a conclusion for location of the project by using DCF techniques. The company needs your comment for making an investment decision

It is assumed that the company will borrow from the market is 250 lakhs.

Profit/Loss before Interest and Depreciation (Rs. in Lakhs)

Year	*Forward Area*	*Backward Area*	*Pv Factor 15 per cent*
1	(5.5)	(55.00)	0.87
2	36.00	(25.00)	0.76
3	56, 00	10.00	0.66
4	76.00	22.00	0.57
5	110.00	47.00	0.50
6	144.00	102.00	0.43
7	158.00	156.00	0.38
8	232.00	192.00	0.33
9	332.00	232.00	0.28
10	432.00	332.00	0.25

Solution:

As per the financial information given in the problem, the solution will requires two steps. Step 1 is to examine the surplus available if the project is located in backward area. The second step needs to study the consequences, if it is located in forward area. Hence, the beneficial to the company will be preferred to locate the factor.

Statement Showing the Net Present Value of the Project at 15 per cent Forward Area

1	2	3	4	5	6	7	8	9	10	11	12
0	—	—	—	—	—	—	—	100	-100	1.00	-100
1	-5.5	35	30	-70.5	—	-70.5	—	35	-35	0.87	-30.45
2	36	35	30	-29	—	-20	10	—	10	0.76	7.6
3	56	35	30	-9	—	—	35	—	35	0.66	23.1
4	76	35	30	11	—	+11	56	62.5	—	0.57	—
5	110	35	22.5	52.5	—	52.5	87.5	62.5	25	0.50	12.5
6	144	35	15.0	94	47	47	82	62.5	19.5	0.43	8.385
7	232	35	7.5	115.5	58	58	93	62.5	30.5	0.38	11.59
8	332	35	0	197	99	99	134	—	134	0.33	44.22
9	332	35	0	297	149	149	184	—	184	0.28	51.52
10	432	35	0	397	198	198	233	—	233	0.25	58.25

+217.165
–130.450

Net Present Value +86.7

Column 1= year
Column 2=profit/loss before interest and depreciation
Column 3=depreciation
Column 4=interest
Column 5=profit/loss after depreciation
Column 6=income tax @ 50%
Column 7=profit after tax
Column 8=cash inflows
Column 9= net outflows (investment operating losses and loan repayment)
Column 10=present cash flows
Column 11= discounted value factor 15%
Column 12= value of cash flows

Statement Showing Net Present Value of Project Located in Backward Area

1	2	3	4	5	6	7	8	9	10	11	12
0	—	—	—	—	—	—	—	85	-85	1.00	-85
1	-55	35	25	-115	—	-115	—	-80	-80	0.87	-69.6
2	-25	35	25	-85	—	-85	—	-50	-50	0.76	-38
3	10	35	25	-50	—	-50	—	-15	-15	0.66	-9.9
4	22	35	25	-38	—	-38	—	62.5	-62.5	0.57	-35.625
5	47	35	18.75	-6.75	—	-6.75	35	62.5	27.5	0.50	13.75
6	102	35	12.50	+55.5	—	+55.5	90.5	62.5	28	0.43	12.04
7	156	35	6.25	114.75	—	114.75	149.75	62.5	62.75	0.38	23.845
8	192	35	—	157	42.25	114.75	149.75	—	149.75	0.33	49.4175
9	232	35	—	197	82.25	114.75	149.75	—	149.75	0.28	41.93
10	332	35	—	297	182.25	114.75	149.75	—	149.75	0.25	37.4375
											(+) 178.42 -239.125= – 60.75

The Net Present Value of Project in Forward Area is +86.75. But the Project in Backward Area Shows a Negative Result of -60.75. Hence Project in Forward Area should be Selected.

Illustration No. 27

ABC Industries Limited provides the following information. The missing information related to the project should be calculated with the given data.

	Particulars	*Rs.*
1.	Life of the machine	4 years
2.	Annual cost saving	50,000
3.	Scrap value	0
4.	Internal rate of return	15 per cent
5.	Profitability index	1.075
6.	Net present value	?
7.	Investment of the project	?
8.	Cost of capital	?
9.	Payback period	?

The cumulative present values of the discount factor for 4 years is as follows:

At 15% 2.855, at 14% 2.913, at 13% 2.974, at 12% 3.038.

Solution: As per the data given, the cost of capital, npv, investment amount of the project and payback period should be calculated.

The project cost can be calculated as follows:

The savings per annum	Rs. 50, 000
Life of the machine	4 years
Internal rate of return	15 per cent

The project internal rate of return is 15 per cent therefore, the cash inflows for 4 years is 50,000.

Considering cumulative discount factor is to be 2.855.

50,000 x 2.855 = 1,42,750

The cost of the project is Rs. 1,42,750

The payback period of the project will be calculated as follows:

Payback period = Initial investment/annual savings

= 1,42,750/50,000 = 2.855

The cost of the capital can be calculated as follows:

With the help of profitability index, we can calculate cost of the capital of the project. Profitability index of the project is 1.075.

If the profitability index were one, cash inflows and outflows would be equal. Therefore 1.075, the cash inflows would be more by 0.075 than outflow.

Profitability index PI = Discounted cash inflows/cost of the project

1.075 = Discounted cash inflows/1,42,750

Or

1.075 x 1, 42,750 = 1, 53,456

The annual cost saving is Rs. 50,000. Hence the cumulative discount factor for 4 years

1,53,456/50,000 = 3.069

The discount factor at 12 per cent, the cumulative discount factor for 4 years is 3.038; therefore, the cost of capital would be 12 per cent.

The net present value of the project

n.p.v. = Total present value of cash inflows–cost of the project
1, 53,456-1, 42,750 = 10,706

Illustration No. 28

Beta Engineering Limited is contemplating to purchase of a new machine to replace the old machine from its factory. The following information is available for consideration:

The company has utilized the old machine since 5 years. The income tax rate is 50 per cent and there is no interest cost.

Particulars	*Old Machine*	*New Machine*
Investment of the machine	50,000	65,000
Life of the machine	10 years	10 years
Selling price per unit	1.40	1.40
Material cost per unit	0.60	0.60
Machine running hours per annum	2,200	2,200
Units per hour	20	30
Power per annum	1800	4200
Stores per annum	6200	7300
Wages per running hour	2.75	5.00
All other charges per annum	7500	8500

The depreciation has to be charged on straight-line method. As per the data given, you are required to calculate the accounting rate of return of the project and suggest which machine is preferable.

Solution:

EVOLUATION OF OLD MACHINE FOR COMPUTATION OF ACCOUNTING RATE OF RETRUN

(a) accounting rate of return = average net earnings/original investment × 100

(b) accounting rate of return= average net earnings/average investment ×100

(c) accounting rate of return=incremental earnings/ incremental investment × 100

Accounting rate of return can be calculated through the above formulas for the given machine. For this purpose, profitability statement should be drawn to provide a meaning full explanation.

Particulars		*Rs.*
Investment of the machine		50,000
Life of the machine		10 years
Production 2200 x 22		48,400
Sales		60,500
Less:		
Direct material 48400 x 0.60	29,040	
Wages 2200 x.2.75	6,050	
Power	1,800	
Stores	6,200	
Other charges	7,500	
Depreciation	5,000	55,590
Profit before tax		4910
Income tax at 50%		2455
Profit after tax		2455

Accounting rate of return=4910/50, 00x100=9.82%
Account rate of return=4910/25,000x100=19.64 %

Accounting rate of return = 7650-2455=5195/65000-25,000x100 =5195/40000x100=12.9%

Evoluation of Profitability Statement of New Machine

Particulars			*Rs*
Investment of the machine			65,000
Life of the machine			10 years
Production 2200 x 30			66000
Sales 66000 x 1.40 =		92,400	
Less: Cost of sales			
Material 66 000 x 0.60 =	39600		
Wages 2200 x 5 =	11000		

Power	4200	
Stores	7300	
Other charges	8500	
Depreciation	6500	77,100
Profit before tax	15,300	
-Tax	7,650	

Profit after tax	7,650	

Accounting rate of return=7650/65,000 x 100=11.76
Accounting rate of return=7,650/32500 x 100=23.57

Therefore, the following result is arrived for making a decision.

The old machine provides arr-i, 9.82, arr-ii, 19.64, arr-iii, 12.0% respectively.

The new machine provide arr-i, 11.76%, arr-ii, 23.57%.

Hence, it is better to replace the old machine because it provides more earnings inflow.

Illustration No. 29

Srinadh Industries Ltd. provides the following information regarding two alternative machines X and Y. You are required to calculate the accounting rate of return.

Particulars	*Machine X*	*Machine Y*
Initial investment	65,000	65,000
Additional investment		
Working capital	6,000	7,000
Life of the machine	5 years	5 years
Scrap value	4,000	4,000
Income tax	55%	55%

Annual Income after Depreciation and Tax

Year	*Inflow*	*Inflow*
1	3,500	7,500
2	4,500	6,500
3	5,500	5,500
4	6,500	4,500
5	7,500	3,500
	-----------	-----------
	27,500	27,500
	-----------	-----------

The company has adopted to charge the depreciation on straight-line basis.

Solution:

Calculation of accounting rate of return
ARR = Annual earnings/average investment ×100
Average income=total income/number of years.
Accounting rate of return for machine X
Machine X = 27,500/5=Rs. 5,500
Machine Y = 27,500/5=Rs. 5,500

AVERAGE INVESTMENT

$$\frac{\text{Original investment} - \text{scrap value}}{2} + \text{addl.net working capital} + \text{scrap value}$$

$$\text{Machine X} = \frac{65{,}000\text{-}4{,}000}{2} + 6000 + 4000$$

$$= 30{,}500 + 6000 + 4000 = 40{,}500$$

$$\text{Machine Y} = \frac{65{,}000 - 4{,}000}{2} + 30{,}500 + 7000 + 4000 = 41{,}500$$

Accounting rate of return machine X = 5500/40,500 × 100 = 13.5%
Accounting rate of return machine Y= 5500/41,500 × 100 = 13.25%

Illustration No. 30

Harish Engineering Limited is searching for a project. The following information provides two projects particulars. You are required to select a better project.

Particulars Cash inflows Year	*Project A*	*Project B*
0	-15000	-15000
1	6000	6000
2	6000	6000
3	3000	3000

The risk less discount rate is 5 per cent. Project A is less risky as compared to project B. The management of the company intends to consider risk premium rates at 5 per cent and 10 per cent respectively.

Solution:

The risk-adjusted discount rate
Project A 5% + 5% = 10%
Project B 5% + 10% = 15%

Calculation of net Present Value of Cash Inflows of two Projects

Year	*Discounted*			*Cash*	*Inflow*	
	PV Project A (10%)			*Project B*	*(15%) PV*	
0			-15,000			-15,000
1	0.91	6.000	5460	6,000	0.87	5220
2	0.83	6,000	4980	6,000	0.76	4560
3	0.75	3,000	2250	3,000	0.66	1980
			-2310			-3240

Both of these two projects generate negative results.

3

Capital Structure

The business enterprise needs money to run the business without any interruption. For smooth functioning of the business enterprise finance play an important role in the company. The funds are required for establishment of the company. The promoters are responsible for making all financial decisions at the time of promotion of the company. They should plan; organize the company in a good manner to overcome of the financial problems. Several companies are facing finance problems and they are unable to run efficiently irrespective of their talent and skills. Financial crunch in the company may pull down the company spirit and ambitions. The organizational goals will only be achieved with a correct estimate of the current and future needs of capital. The sufficient funds resources will help the company to work without any stress and ambiguity. The accurate estimation of funds depends upon the company's managerial and financial capabilities. The business requires a lot of guesswork. The guesswork will be possible with a rich and varied experience in that field. The procurement of funds is the basic task of financial manager. The basic objective of financial management is wealth maximization. It can be achieved with a good planning of financial resources. The finance manager of the company should always think about the wealth maximization of the firm by adopting good techniques for raising of financial resources. He must also to look after the resources in a better utilization method. Therefore, the finance manager should design a good combination for raising of finance through different financial instruments from the capital market. Capital market is always providing finance for the corporate sector. The finance manager should estimate the requirement of present and future financial resources and design the financial combination in order to reach the goal of the firm. He should keep the welfare of the shareholders and always try to raise the finance with low cost fund sources. However, the cost of capital or financial resources must be in low cost. A low cost of availability of funds may boost up the profitability of the firm. The total requirement of financial resources may be mobilized through different sources of financial instrument. The mix of various financial combinations is known as capital structure. Capital structure can be described as a good ingredient in foodstuff. It can be called as chemistry of finance. It also may be described as cocktail of a good wine. A good wine will provide best taste only when it is mixed in a right mix of combination. The proportion of various financial instruments may create wealth in the company. The creation of wealth is possible with only good capital structure. The business needs long and short-term sources of finance. The requirement of long-term finance may be procured through equity shares, preference shares, debentures, bonds, internal resources, and other sources of finance. Short-term finance may be fulfilled through commercial banks short-term loans, supplier's credit, debentures, bank overdraft, and from money market. There is no rule for mobilization of resources for long-term or short-term. There is no ideal formula for designing capital structure of a firm. This is because of varying circumstances of various business undertakings. The capital structure depends upon number of factors. The gestation period, the nature of the product, certainty in business sector is highly influential factors in designing of the capital structure. The banking sector, government policies, fiscal and monetary policies will also influencing the designing of capital structure. However, the finance manager shouid keep in mind about the welfare of the shareholders. He should always search for a cheaper cost of funds and better utilization of resources. The funds must be utilized in a productive way. Any misuse of financial resources will not be accepted by the law. The capital structure is made up of debt and equity. It provides long-term sources of financing to the company.

Capital structure is a qualitative aspect of the business enterprise. It deals with the better utilization of financial resources and low cost of funds. Generally, the corporate sector will raise their long-term sources of finance through three sources. They are equity, preference, and debentures. The finance manager should design good proportion of this combination of different financial instruments. The combination of different financial instruments will be followed by the corporate sector as follows:

(a) Equity shares only.
(b) Equity and preference shares.
(c) Equity share and debenture.
(d) Equity shares, preference shares, and debentures.

IMPORTANCE OF CAPITAL STRUCTURE

The capital structure refers to the relationships between various long-term sources of finance. It deals with the advantages and disadvantages of the different kinds of financial instruments available in the market. It is useful and helpful in wealth creation of the company. A proper mix of different financial instruments will definitely yield better results to the corporate sector. Generally, good reputed companies will have higher financial raising capacity from the market. *For example,* ICICI bank is going for capital market for raising of Rs. 20,000 crores from the market. It is a mega issue. DLF Company is also raised huge financial resources from the market. The issue of equity has subscribed more than 3 times. The company is related to real estate group. Therefore, well–reputed and high brand image organizations can raise financial resources from the market according to their needs and convenient. At present private equity boom is more popular in the market. Private equity means, a range of transactions and or assets fall under its purview, including venture capital investments, leveraged buyouts, and mezzanine debt financing, where the creditor expects to gain from the appreciation in equity value by exploiting conversion features such as rights, warrants, or options. Special funds created to finance such investments have a long history.

Various authors defined the term capital structure in different ways. According to some authors in financial management, capital structure is consists of both long and short-term sources of finance. The finance student should know the difference between capitalization, financial structure, and capital structure. Capitalization means the total amount of securities issued by the company. It is a quantitative aspect of the financial planning of the company. Financial structure is related to study about a specified percentage of short-term debt, long-term debt, and shareholder's funds. It may be described as total financial resources marshaled by the firm in the business. It includes short as well as long-term and all forms of debt as well as equity.

Finance is the most important and influencing factor in business decision-making process. Financé provides liberty to the company for executing the business transaction in very smoothly and fastly. Financing the firm's assets is a crucial role in business affairs. In the world of finance, there is a general rule; every business enterprise should be used finance in a proper mix of debt and equity. Debt is necessary for business enterprise like death is to human being. Debt is an important and most influencing factor in all business decisions of the corporate sector. Debt requires a payment of fixed cost to the owner of the fund. The fund is a available in the financial markets at always for a fixed rate of cost. Well good-reputed firms can raise financial resources from the market at 24x7 bases. The Indian capital market has strong absorbing capacity for the requirement of corporate sector's financial needs. Preference share capital is also part of the capital structure. Preference share capital requires a fixed rate of dividend to the owners. Dividend is a reward to the investor. Interest payment is a recurring expenditure to the business enterprise. The expenditure incurred by the corporate sector towards fund utilization is known as advantage. Debt and death is necessary for everyone. The cost towards funds is made by the company is known as financial cost. Financial cost is one of the components in total cost of product. Any increase in financial cost component leads to force the company to increase selling price. Selling price increase leads to a shortfall of sales volumes. Therefore the margin of the company under pressure. A decrease in sales volume will paralyze the business organization. At present environment, no company has dared to increase the selling price due to heavy competition in the market. Market is a combination of different factors and elements. There will be several players in the market and everyone organization move more cautiously. All the business organizations are rotating towards profit element. Profit is oxygen to the commercial enterprise. It is the lifeblood of a business organization. Every business organization tries to reduce the expenses and to increase profits. Profit earning is the barometer for measuring the efficiency of a business enterprise. Competition in the market makes to careful analysis of the expenses incurred by the corporate sector. Generally, the corporate sector needs financial resources in two occasions: (a) expansion, (b) diversification. Expansion and diversification situations create a huge amount of financial resources commitment on the part of the business enterprise. It is a thumb rule that, when a company raises financial resources, the company should pay interest or dividend to the fund suppliers. Therefore, the company should earn more than the financial cost of the fund. Hence, the shareholders will get benefit. *For example,* a company has an equity capital of Rs. 10 consists of 10,000 shares.

The shares are fully paid up. The total amount of capital is Rs.1,00,000. The company earns profit approximately Rs. 40, 000. In this situation, the company is going to expand its activities. It requires an additional amount of finance Rs.1,00,000. Hence, the company has two alternatives either to borrow the finance or mobilize from share market by issue of shares. However, the company should earn sufficient profit to meet this additional fund cost. This situation will show impact on the earning per share of the company. A higher amount of profit may help to stimulate the higher level of eps or otherwise the eps will be in more pressure. The margins will be under pressure and a high debt component in the capital structure leads to become insolvency.

OPTIMUM CAPITAL STRUCTURE

The finance manager occupies a dominant role in designing of the capital structure of a business enterprise. The designing of capital structure is a difficult task before financial manager. He should keep always in mind about the welfare of the shareholders. He is the custodian of the shareholders of the company. He should take a good decision that will greatly show impact on earnings of the company. Wealth maximization is the most important factor before the finance manager while designing the capital structure of the company. A good design of capital structure is known as optimum capital structure. The optimum capital structure should enhance the profitability levels of the company. A good debt and equity mix is known as optimum capital structure. However, it is a difficult task to design optimum capital structure because of some internal and external factors in the business environment. A fall in market value of the company depends upon many factors. Stock market is a highly volatile and no one can expect the fluctuations. The fall in market value of the share will greatly show impact on the capital structure. An increase in high debt leads to risk. In theoretical approach, we can speak a lot on capital structure but in practice, it is not quite possible. However, the optimum capital structure has the following features:

(a) Earning capability
(b) Time
(c) Control
(d) Liquidity

(a) *Earning Capability*: Profit is the basic aim of all business enterprises. The earning profit through business activities will be reflected the efficiency of a business enterprise. Competition in the market, it forces all the companies to reduce their selling price. Every company wants to minimize the cost and maximize the profit. The welfare of the shareholder is most important to all the business enterprises. Generally, every company is interested to reduce cost of production and increase their profitability. The cost of production is a combination of prime cost, factory cost, administrative cost, office cost, financial cost, and selling and distribution cost. The cost components will influence the final selling price of the product. Hence, the financial cost is also considered as input cost in arriving the final product cost. Therefore, the financial manager needs to a careful design of capital structure. Capital structure is a composition of equity and debt. The business will be run by either borrowed or own funds. The borrowed will consists of long-term loans from financial institutions, banks, issue of debentures, issue of bonds, etc., own funds in the company consists of large pool amount of reserves, surplus amount, retention of undistributed profits, amortization funds. The combination of owned and borrowed funds needs payment of cost. The finance manager should think about the cost of funds. He should always think about the cheaper rate of interest cost and maximize the welfare of the shareholders.

(b) *Time*: The finance manager role is to minimize the cost and maximize the welfare of the shareholders. The business needs money to earn money. The top-level management will frame the investment of the company. The finance manager is responsible to explain the various sources of finance and explain the advantages and disadvantages of the various alternatives. As per the designing of the capital structure, the company is required to approach financial markets to raise their financial resources. Financial markets are always available to the good reputed and sincere companies. The markets are available on 24×7 bases. The large and reputed companies can raise financial resources at any time. However, the small and medium size companies are unable to raise their resources from the market at all time. Financial markets are consisting of money market and capital market. These markets are depend upon various factors from time-to-time. The capital structure designed by the company should enable the organization to approach the financial market whenever the need arises.

(c) *Control*: The finance manager should design the capital structure to face any kind of risk that exists in the markets. He should take a cautious approach for the welfare of the shareholders. The capital structure should be useful to the company like a cushion, which is helpful to absorb any kind of unforeseen events. The business consists of threats and opportunities. Business opportunities are created primarily by three major things shortages in an economy, major changes in demographics and global disruptions.

(d) *Liquidity*: The finance manager should keep in mind while designing its capital structure. The welfare of shareholders is most important factor. Capital structure is a reflection of borrowed and own funds. He should maintain the company liquidity by avoiding unnecessary debts. Debt is not a luxury it is a costly affair. If the company is able to generate sufficient profits then the debt is not a luxury and costly affair. The fundamental principle of financial management says that the debt should be in a position to generate adequate margins. In this juncture, rising of debt is not a mistake or crime. A reasonable cost is to be payable to the owner of the fund. If a company is able to earn more amount of profits with little amount of debt then it is good decision. However, the company should be able to repay the debt content when the fund supplier demands. The payment of debt along with its interest is known as liquidity. Every company should make liquidity levels. Maintenance of liquidity levels stimulates the goodwill of the company.

FACTORS DETERMINING CAPITAL STRUCTURE

The finance manager is a key person in designing capital structure of the company. The board of directors will discuss about the capital structure of the company with a reference made by the financial manager. Hence the financial manager should keep all factors about the company while designing the capital structure. Capital structure planning aims at the maximization of profits and minimization of cost. The financial manager should make efforts to better utilization of debt. The debt should be used for a productive way. In this situation, the company's welfare will be fulfilled. The management of a business enterprise should try to reach as near as possible of the optimum point of debt and equity mix.

The capital structure of a company depends upon a several factors. These factors are presented for a detailed discussion to make way that is more meaningful.

1. Trading on equity or leverage
2. Sales volume
3. Cost of fund
4. Absorbing capacity
5. Product nature
6. Sector of the company
7. Control
8. Flexibility
9. Desires of investors
10. Market position
11. Composition of assets
12. Statutory requirements
13. Monetary and fiscal policies

1. *Trading on Equity or Advantage*: Business needs money to earn money. Money always rotates around money. Money is chased by money. Therefore, investment is necessary for any kind of business enterprise to make profits. Profits are highly influential and not avoidable factor in boardroom decisions. The finance manager should make a good combination of debt and ownership funds to reach the goal of a business enterprise. The business will be run with borrowed and owned fund. However, these deployed financial

resources commands cost. The cost is known as advantage. Advantage means ability to pay expenses by the firm in executing the business operations. Financial advantage means, the cost of funds to be borne by the company for deployment in the business. The capital structure of a company consists with high debt component, and then the company is required to pay in the form of interest to the fund suppliers. The fund suppliers are interested towards their interest amount. They are outsiders of the company and no ways concerned with the ownership of the business enterprise. The component of owned fund consists of large amount of reserves, equity share capital, preference share capital, undistributed profits, and amortized funds. The use of borrowed fund and owned funds will reflect on the earning per share of the company. Debt is a component, which provides tax benefits. As per the income-tax act, payment of interest is treated as business expenditure and it is entitled to get deduction from the taxable profit. Preference shareholders are entitled to get a fixed rate of dividend on their fund. A fixed amount of dividend is liable to pay to the fund suppliers. They are owners of the company but not in a position to participate in business decisions. The dividend paid to the shareholders is not treated as business expenditure and hence there is no chance to claim income-tax exemption. The equity shareholders are the real owners of the company and they provide large amount of resources for the reward of either dividend or capital appreciation. The equity shareholders are more powerful than other fund suppliers are. A high content of equity in the capital structure will definitely influence the company earning per share. Generally, equity shareholders will have more expectations from the company. They supply fund for a better reward. They are highly influencing people and the company has to show its performance as per the expectations of the shareholders, otherwise the company will face severe financial problems. The use of different components in capital structure will definitely show impact on earning per share of the company. If a company earns sufficient profits with the help of borrowed funds, then there will be positive impact on earning per share of the company. If the company fails to earn reasonable profits in order to meet its financial cost, then there will be negative impact on earning per share

2. *Sales Volume*: Sales are most important and influencing factor in business. A higher sales volume may generate more profits. A

hefty amount of profit will keep happy the shareholders of the company. A stable growth in sales enables the company to raise finance through debt instrument. A strong stable sale ensures the company for smooth functioning of the business activities without any interruption. This situation is helpful to the company for payment of fixed interest cost to the fund suppliers. If the company faces shortfall in sales, it is better to maintain the capital structure with low content of debt.

3. *Cost of Funds*: The financial resources are available in the market for a fixed rate of interest as per the market movement. The borrowed fund is useful to the company when the business enterprise generates more than the cost of fund and keeps the company with surplus money. If the company fails to earn below the rate of interest cost of funds, then the business organization should drop from these activities. Hence, it is more important factor while raising debt financial resources from the market. The main sources of finance for a corporate entity are equity, preference, debentures, and bonds. Debt is a generally cheapest source of finance. The payment of interest will be treated as business expenditure and tax exemption is available to the company. There will be legal obligation for payment of interest and redemption of principal amount within a stipulated period. Strong and stable sales will keep happy situation to the company for payment of interest and redemption of the principal amount. Equity is another source of finance to the corporate world. Generally, equity is jam and debt is ginger to the corporate sector. Equity shareholders are real owners of the company. It is not a legal obligation to pay the dividend to the shareholders. Hence, the company has an advantage this situation, when the company fails to earn sufficient profits. It provides flexibility to the company and the shareholders will wait for reward. Preference share capital is a combination of equity and debt, because as debt, it requires a regular payment of dividend and the amount of capital should be refunded within period. Hence, there will be pressure on financial resources of the company at the time of refund or redeeming the principal amount. However, equity share capital is the permanent sources of finance to the company. There is no redemption for the equity and it will be refunded only at the time of winding up of the company. Therefore, the financial resource of the company, which is available in the form of equity, is best sources for long-term utilization of

the company business. A company can utilize these cost free fund towards in a better way to enrich the shareholders. Equity is like a shock absorber to smooth functioning of the company. The prosperity of the shareholders will be stimulated when the funds are utilized in a productive manner. While designing the capital structure, the finance manager should keep in mind regarding all aspects of advantages and disadvantages of various alternatives prevailing in the market.

4. *Absorbing Capacity*: A good and well–reputed companies will enjoy the brand loyalty. A strong brand loyalty will generate a higher amount of sales. A growth in sales makes the company more confident to pay fixed amount of interest within time schedules. A large amount of debt is also may not be harmful to the company because of brand loyalty. In this situation, the company should verify various ratios to satisfy liquidity position of the company.

5. *Nature of Product*: The capital structure of the company depends upon nature of the product, which the company produce and sell in the market. Usually the companies, which cannot provide stable earnings due to the nature of the product, will have relied on equity share capital. Public utilities like electricity, power generation, transport organizations require more debt component in their capital structure. Manufacturing companies will require a higher amount of capital on long-term basis. These companies should rely more on equity capital. Small companies will have depended upon equity capital because they are unable to procure long-term debts from the market.

6. *Sector of the Company*: Generally, the market is divided into two kinds. They are monopoly and competitive markets. The monopoly firms will greatly rely on debentures and preference shares. The competitive market firms will go for issue of equity for their financial requirement. Usually the monopoly companies will enjoy the stable and growth in sales.

7. *Control*: The corporate world is based on democratic system of pattern. The real owners of the company are equity shareholders. The board of directors is elected from the shareholders. The corporate sector boardrooms are elected and the day-to-day affairs will be looking after by the managing director. The issue of equity capital enables the company to invite new shareholders. The existing management wants to retain the control with them and

there will be a chance for arising to boardroom battles. There are several boardroom battles exist in Indian corporate sector. Hence, the existed management is not interested to go for issue of new shares due to a threat to their company control. In these situations, the companies generally prefer to go for issue of debentures for their financial needs.

8. *Flexibility*: The capital structure of the business enterprise should be flexible. The efficiency of the financial manager will be recognized in the designing of flexible capital structure. The company should be able to face any situation commanded by the business environment. The business enterprises are rotating towards profit. Profit is always chased by several organizations. In this chasing of profit environment, only the efficient companies will reach the goal. The company should be able to raise its additional fund in a changing business environment. The changing business scenario dictates terms to the corporate sector. In this situation, the company should be flexible to raise its financial needs from the market. The company should design its capital structure to meet the changing environment. According to the flexibility of the company, redeemable preference shares and debentures may be preferred. The company may also depend upon preference shares and debentures, which provide highest flexibility to the business enterprise.

9. *Desires of the Investors*: The corporate sector will fulfill their financial needs through either equity or borrowed funds. Equity is the permanent source of capital. Fund suppliers from the capital market supply borrowed funds. Funds are available at a fixed rate of interest in the market according to the situation based on demand and supply. Every commodity in the business is based on a simple logic demand and supply. Therefore, if the company is showing interest towards debt it can be raised from institutions and private investors. Institutional investors are in an organized sector. The private investors are general investors. Generally, the investors can be classified as three types, (a) risk investors, (b) cautious investor's, (c) risk free investors. The risk baring investors are called as courageous investors. They are ready to face any risk arising from their investment. They will accept any type of situation regarding their investment. It is a fundamental principle of financial management that, a high-risk financial instrument yields more return, a low risk of financial instrument may generate lower

returns, a risk free financial instrument will generate a little amount of returns. Therefore, the return is based on acceptance of investor's risk perception. High-risk investors will generally prefer to invest in equity share capital. These kinds of investors will undertake all kinds of risk. Cautious investors may put their investments in debentures. Risk free investors will put their investment in preference share capital.

10. *Market Position*: The market is a combination of different factors. The market is based on supply and demand factors of the funds. The capital market is consisting with fund suppliers and borrowers. The funds are always available in the market for a cost. The capital structure of the corporate sector will be influenced by the market sentiments. The market will pass on different movements. Some times the investors in the market will think about the safety of their investment, in this situation there will be crazier for debentures issues. At this moment, the corporate sector will go for debentures issue for their financial requirements. If the market is interested towards speculative buying then it is better to go for equity issues. The investors will generally respond according to the market sentiments. Hence, the companies before going to take a capital structure decision, they must keep in mind about the market sentiment, and otherwise the issue may not become successful.

11. *Composition of Assets*: Designing of capital structure is the most important task of the financial manager. The company will reflect the skills utilized by the financial manager in the manner of profit booking. While designing the capital structure of the company, the financial manager should keep about the liquidity position of the company. Liquidity is the most important factor, which cannot be ignored by the company. Liquidity creates good reputation. Good reputation of the company enhances the sales of the product. The enhanced sales will generate more profit. The increased profit will make to make shareholders happy. The business enterprises will generally invest in different composition of assets. If the company invest more amounts in fixed assets, it is better to raise the financial resources by way of equity.

12. *Statutory Requirement*: The financial manager will design the capital structure and he will get the approval of the board of directors and shareholders. If the proposal suggest, the issue of share capital then the promoters should follow several legal

formalities as per the provisions of the companies. The capital market is looking after by the securities and exchange board of India. SEBI is the powerful organ in the capital market. Every company before approaching capital market, it should apply at first to the SEBI. After completion of all SEBI formalities, the company can enter into capital market for raising of financial resources from the public. All public issues in India should get the approval of the SEBI. SEBI is the watchdog of Indian stock market. Hence, the company should keep all factors while designing its capital structure.

13. *Monetary and Fiscal Policies*: Government policies in business environment will occupy a dominant role in decision-making. The corporate sector has no liberty to move as per its convenience. Policy is a long-term nature of the behaviour. Government policy is an influencing and important factor in the designing of capital structure. The Reserve Bank of India is supreme authority in lending policy of financial institutions. The Bank will change its policy from time-to-time. A change in policy of lending financial institutions will completely modify the pattern. A change in SEBI rules will arise. The issuing company has to submit several documents to the SEBI in order to satisfy the government rules and regulations.

Hence, planning of capital structure involves several factors, which influences the financial plan of the company. However, the financial manager should take all precautions and get the necessary approvals from various parties in order to execute the financial plan. He should closely observe the relation between borrowed and own capital. The relationship between borrowed and own capital is known as "Capital Gearing." Capital gearing reveals the relationship between equity capital and long-term debt. The composition or ratio between equity and long-term debt may be planned or historical. However, at present situation the finance manager should verify if whether the company is in high gear or low gear. If the company raises most of its funds through long-term debt then the company is in high gear, otherwise it will be in low gear. Low gear stands for higher proportion of equity and lower proportion of long-term debt. Therefore, the problem of gearing ratio will show impact on company profitability. If the company is in low gearing ratio, dividend should be paid to the shareholders. Because in low gearing ratio, the equity composition will be high and a higher rate of the shareholders expect dividend.

Therefore, there will be a pressure on divisible profits. The company is always thinking about to satisfy the company shareholders. The shareholders will satisfy when the company declares a higher rate of dividend or otherwise they will be in dissatisfaction. If the company is in high gear ratio, it consists of large amount of long-term debt, then the company will have to pay fixed rate of interest in larger amount. The earning capability of the company will be swallowed by financial cost. Therefore maintaining of balanced capital gearing is most important task before the company management. Capital gearing is not affecting only shareholders, but also debenture holders, financial institutions, and creditors. The capital gearing will utilized as a tool, if the company utilizes it intelligently. It can be used by the corporate sector during various phases of business trade cycles. Inflation and deflations are most common factors in the economy. Inflation means, a rise in price levels of all commodities and services, which exist in the market. If the economy is in inflation, it is better to follow high gear policy. During the inflation period, generally, the corporate sector will earn higher profits and it can easily meet its fixed financial cost. In the deflation period, the company earnings are low and it is unable to meet its fixed cost, therefore the company should be in low gear position.

Alteration of Capital Structure: Capital structure is an important and influencing factor in financial management of the corporate sector. However, there are no hard rules and regulations for good capital structure. The capital structure once decided by the company is not a permanent structure. It will be altered according to the financial needs of the company. The expansion, growth, revision, diversification will make the company to alter its capital structure. The changes in capital structure may be either voluntary or compulsory in order to meet its present situation. The following factors will necessitate the company to alter the balancing capital structure.

1. Simplify
2. Reduction of deficit
3. Obligations
4. Reduction of dividend
5. Merger
6. Retention

1. *Balancing*: Capital structure of the company is not a permanent factor. It can be altered as per the needs and convenience to the company. However, the financial manager should keep in mind the welfare of the shareholders while altering its capital structure. If the company involved in heavy amount of borrowed funds, it may readjust by issue of equity and debt will be redeemed. This situation will favour to the company and a lot of pressure on profits will be reduced. Hence, the alteration of capital structure will be utilized as a weapon to readjust the financial pressures on the company.

2. *Reduction*: If the company is not functioning properly, it is better to re-organize the capital structure of the company. There will be a difference between book value of assets and real worth of assets of the company. If the assets are overvalued as per book value then the company, should reorganize the capital and reduce the book value of its liabilities and assets.

3. *Obligations*: An alteration in capital structure needs legal fulfillment of various acts and regulations from time-to-time in force. The corporate sector is required to fulfill legal formalities under several acts.

4. *Reduction of Accumulated Dividend*: Generally, companies will issue two kinds of shares, (i) Equity, (ii) Preference shares. Equity shareholders are real owners and risk averse people. Preference shareholders are fund suppliers for a fixed rate of dividend for their commitment. They are not interested in taking risk in investment. They are entitled to get a fixed rate of dividend in every year until their amount of redemption. If the company is not in a position to pay dividend to its preference shareholders, then the company will raise financial resources through equity shares and the preference share capital amount will be redeemed. Hence, there is no pressure on profits for payment of preference shareholders dividend.

5. *Mergers:* Merger and acquisition is one of the important phenomenons in corporate sector. Mergers will be arising in several situations. Expansion is another important factor in the life of the company. If the business is increased beyond its levels then the companies will go for expansion process. In this situation, the corporate sector will readjust their capital structure.

6. *Retention*: The dividend policy of the company will make a demarcation between divisible profits and retention profits. The

earnings of the company should belonged to the owners of the company. Generally, the corporate sector will retain some amount of profits to run the business smoothly. If the company wants to keep the heavy profit with it, then it should issue bonus shares. Bonus shares are paper profits. The company will retain the cash position and the shareholders enjoy shares. Bonus shares will be issued in lie of dividend. Hence, the issue of bonus shares will alter the capital structure of the company.

THEORIES OF CAPITAL STRUCTURE

The value of a business enterprise depends upon its earning capacity. Business is a combination of deployment of financial and human resources. Every business enterprise will try to minimize the risk and maximize return for the welfare of shareholders. The deployment of financial resources in business commands financial cost. The financial cost will show an impact on the efficiency of the firm. There is a strong relationship between cost of capital and capital structure. The financial resources, which are available in the capital market, command a fixed rate of cost that depends upon from time-to-time. The capital market is a combination of fund suppliers and fund borrowers. The funds are available at an agreed price that depends upon demand and supply position of the financial resources. The company should take a careful decision about the mobilization of financial resources. There are different kinds of capital structure theories exist in the practice; different authors define them in different ways. The following are important theories of capital structure:

1. Net Income Approach
2. Net Operating Income Approach
3. The Traditional Approach
4. Modigliani and Miller Approach

The theories of capital structure are based on the following assumptions:

(a) There are two sources of financial resources only, *i.e.,* debt and capital.
(b) There are no corporate taxes.

(c) The dividend payout ratio is 100 per cent.
(d) Permanent capital structure, there is no scope for alteration.
(e) The business risk remains constant.
(f) The earning capacity before tax and interest is constant.
(g) The firm has a strong and stable life.
(h) The investment decisions of the firm is stable.

1. *Net Income Approach*: This approach was based on the works of *David Durand*. According to this approach, the capital structure decision will influence the value of the firm. A change in capital structure of the firm will show impact on overall cost of capital which reflect in the total value of the commercial enterprise. According to this approach, debt can be used as a tool to enhance the value of the firm. The debt component will be increased in order to reduce the overall cost of capital. It is based on the following assumptions:

(i) Debt is cheapest sources of finance than equity.
(ii) There are no corporate taxes.
(iii) The risk perception of the investors.

This approach is more beneficial when the financial markets provide the funds at low cost of interest rates. The interest rates are generally monitored by the Reserve Bank of India. The interest amount paid by the corporate sector will attract income-tax exemption to the corporate sector. The value of the business enterprise can be ascertained as follows:

V = S+B
V = Value of firm
S = Market value of equity
B = Market value of debt

The Equity Market Value Can Be Computed As Follows

S = NI/Ke
S = Market value of equity
NI = Net income available to equity shareholders
Ke = Equity capitalization rate

2. *Net Operating Income Approach*: Durand submitted this approach. He says that the market value of the firm will not be influenced by a change in capital structure. It is quite opposite to the net income approach. This theory suggests that a change in capital structure does not affect the market value of the firm and the overall cost of capital will remain constant irrespective of method of financing. Hence, this theory explains that, there is no relation between cost of financial resources and method of financing decision. This approach believes that there is no optimum capital structure exists in the corporate sector and every capital structure is optimum capital structure. This approach assumes the debt equity mix as 50:50 or 20:80 or 0:100. This approach is based on the following assumptions:

(i) There are no corporate taxes.
(ii) The cost of capital remains constant in degrees of debt equity mix ratio.
(iii) The market capitalization of the firm cannot be split between equity and debt component.

In this approach, the value of the firm will be computed as follows:

Market value of the firm (V) = Net Operating Income/Overall Cost of Capital

V = EBIT/KO
Ebit = Earning before interest and taxes
KO = Overall cost of equity
Cost of equity= EBIT-I/V-B
EBIT = Earning Before Intrest And Taxes
I = Interest on Debt
V = Value of The Firm
B = Value of Debt Capital In Capital Structure

3. *The Traditional Approach*: The traditional approach reveals that, the debt should be utilized in a proper way when it is available at low cost of interest. The value of the firm can be stimulated with the help of available cheaper sources of finance. The optimum capital structure can be reached through an ideal debt equity mix. The value of the firm can be enhanced through procuring cheaper source of debt. The deployment of heavy funds through debt is

also not feasible to the corporate sector. Heavy debt in capital structure leads to insolvency of the business enterprise. The traditional approach is also known as intermediate approach. This approach is a compromise between net income and net operating income approach. As per net income approach, the debt content in capital structure of the company is useful to the commercial enterprise. However, the net operating income approach says that the debt content in capital structure of the firm is no relevant to its earning potential. It is irrelevant to the business potential to earn profit. Hence, the traditional approach is a midway to these two approaches.

4. *Modigliani and Miller Approach*: The Modigliani and Miller approach is very popular among capital structure theories. According to its approach, the value of business enterprises is independent and no factor will show impact on earning potential of the commercial enterprise. It is similar to net operating income approach. The M & M approach is based on the following assumptions:

1. There are no corporate taxes.
2. Dividend payout ratio is 100 per cent.
3. The existence of perfect capital market.
4. Investors act rationally.

This approach argues that the weighted average cost of capital does not change with change in the debt equity mix or capital structure of the business enterprise. It strongly believes that the overall cost of capital and the value of firm are independent of the capital structure. They are constant at all levels of debt equity mix. It is based on the idea that no matter how you divide the capital structure of a firm among debt, equity and other claims, there is conservation of investment value. Therefore, the total value of the business enterprise depends upon its underlying profitability and risk. This approach reveals that the profit earned by the commercial enterprise does not demark the profit earned with the help of either equity or debt.

This approach ignores the importance of corporate tax. However, this approach can be analyzed in two situations.

(a) ignoring the corporate tax
(b) considering the corporate tax

(a) *Ignoring the Corporate Tax*: The government levies taxes and it is unavoidable factor in the corporate sector. Tax payment is an obligation. This approach is because the cost of capital is not affected by changes in the capital structure. It strongly argues that the debt equity mix is irrelevant in assessing the total value of the firm. This approach assumes that debt is cheaper to equity. This approach also indicate that beyond a certain limit of debt, the cost of debt increases but the cost of equity falls thereby agaín balancing the two costs.

(b) *Considering Corporate Tax*: Modigliani and Miller indicated that the firm value will increase with the help of high debt content use and cost of capital may be reduced substantially. The use of debt content in the capital structure provides the income tax exemption on payment of interest. The corporate sector is entitled to get income tax exemption on payment of interest to fund suppliers. Therefore, the firm will be benefited through an optimum mix of debt and equity.

M & M approach observed the arbitrate process as an important factor in the capital structure. Arbitrage means, buying of an asset in one market, where it is available for low price and selling it in another market for a higher price level. The difference between two markets is known as profit for the speculator or investor. This approach suggested that two identical firms in all respects except their capital structure could not have different market values due to arbitrage process. If two identical firms except for their capital structure have different market values, arbitrage will take place and the investors will engage in personal advantage than corporate advantage.

Good Capital Structure: Profit is the basic element for any kind of business enterprise. All companies in the market try to sell their produce at low price with high quality. At the present situation, competition in the market is very tough, quality and price only run the show. In order to meet the tough competition, every company is concentrating on cost cutting techniques. Cost is the important factor and influencing element in determining the profit. The earnings profit will be reflect in the market share price of the company. The financial cost will be added to the finished product cost. It is also a part of inner element in determining the selling price. Hence, all companies want to reduce their cost. A good design of capital structure needs many efforts. It is an intellectual process. The following factors should be kept in mind before designing a capital structure of the company.

A. *Minimizes Risk and Maximizes Return:* A good capital structure should be helpful to the company in reducing the cost of product. If the company follows cost reduction programme, it may enhance the profit levels. The financial manager of the company should always try to look after the welfare of the shareholders through earning per share value of the company.
B. *Good Financial Status:* The company capital structure should be designed and can be altered at any time according to the situation but keeping it in good financial status. Goodwill and reputation is an inner element and intangible assets. The design of capital structure should not damage the goodwill and reputation of the company. The insolvency position of the company may spoil the reputation and it ultimately shows impact on sales and profitability of the company. High debt content in capital structure may leads to insolvency position of the company.
C. *Alteration of Capital Structure:* The capital structure of a business enterprise must be constructed according to the convenience and needs of the company. It should be in flexible status. It can be modified whenever the company requires. Hence, the finance manager of the company should design a good capital structure, which may be based on flexibility.
D. *Balance between Debt and Equity:* The company should maintain a balance between debt and equity. A high concentration of debt in the capital structure is more dangerous to the company. A low equity of capital is also not feasible to the commercial enterprise. Equity is a permanent and cheapest source to the corporate sector. Hence, balancing between equity and debt levels is a difficult task before financial experts of the corporate sector.

GRADED ILLUSTRATIONS

Illustration No. 1

Gowthami Industries Ltd. provides the following information. You are required to compute

(a) Capitalization
(b) Capital structure
(b) Financial structure

Liabilities	*Rs.*
Equity	15, 00,000
Preference share capital	7, 50,000
Debentures	3, 00,000
Retained earnings	9, 00,000
Capital surplus	75,000
Current liabilities	2, 25,000
Total	37, 50,000

Solution:

The capitalization of the company can be computed as follows:

Equity share capital	15, 00,000
Preference share capital	7, 50,000
Debentures	3, 00,000
Capitalization	25, 50,000

(ii) *Capital Structure*: It can be computed in two different ways. Some authors in finance area retained earning and capital surplus will be treated as part of the capital structure.

Particulars	*Rs.*	*Proportionate mix*
Equity share capital	15, 00,000	58.82%
Preference share capital	7, 50,000	29.41%
Debentures	3, 00,000	11.77%
Total	25, 50,000	100%

ALTERNATIVE METHOD

Particulars	*Rest*	*Proportionate mix*
Equity share capital	15, 00,000	42.55%
Preference share capital	7, 50,000	21.28%
Debentures	3, 00,000	8.51%
Retained earnings	9, 00,000	25.53%
Capital surplus	75,000	2.13%
Total	35, 25,000	100%

(iii) Financial structure can be computed as follows:

Particulars	*Rs.*	*Proportionate mix*
Equity share capital	15, 00,000	40%
Preference share capital	7, 50,000	20%
Debentures	3, 00,000	8%
Retained earnings	9, 00,000	24%
Capital surplus	75,000	2%
Current liabilities	2, 25,000	6%
Total	37, 50,000	100%

Illustration No. 2

Reliance Industries Limited has a share capital of Rs. 1,50,000 divided into share of Rs. 10 each. The company is searching for better alternative methods for raising of additional Rs. 75,000 financial resources. The following alternatives exist to the management.

(a) Procurement of financial resources by issue of 7500 equity shares of Rs. 10 each.
(b) Mobilizing the resources through issue of 10 per cent preference share capital of Rs. 10 each.
(c) Company intends to issue 8 per cent debentures of Rs. 75,000.

The management of the company needs your advice for better alternative method for mobilizing financial resources. The present earnings of the company are Rs. 60,000 per annum. You are also required to calculate the earning per share after expansion.

(i) Company is earning before interest and tax continues to be same even after the expansion process has been taken.
(ii) The company is earning before interest and tax increases by Rs. 15,000.

Solution:

The above financial information reveals various situations of the financial status. As financial consultant, you are required to calculate the company is earning before interest and tax at different levels.

(i) *Calculation earning per share at present and projected situation of the Reliance Industries Ltd. (EBIT is 60,000)*

Particulars	*Present Capital Structure*	*Proposed* *(i)*	*Capital* *(ii)*	*Structure Situation* *(iii)*
	All equity	all equity	equity+pref.	Equity+ debt
(1)	(2)		(3)	
EBIT	60,000	60,000	60,000	60,000
-Interest	–	–	–	6,000
PBT	60,000	60,000	60,000	54,000
-TAX	30,000	30,000	30,000	27,000
PAT	30,000	30,000	30,000	27,000
-Preference Dividend	–	–	–7,500	–
Profit for equity shareholders	30,000	30,000	22,500	27,000
Number of Equity shares	15,000	22,500	15,000	15,000
EPS	Rs.2	1.33	1.50	1.80

(ii) *Calculation of earning per share when EBIT increases by Rs.15,000*

Particulars	*Present Capital Structure*	*Proposed Capital*		*Structure*
	All Equity	(i) (E)	(ii) (E+P)	(iii) (E+D)
EBIT	60,000	75,000	75,000	75,000
-Interest	-	-	-	6,000
PBT	60,000	75,000	75,000	69,000
-TAX	30,000	37,500	37,500	34,500
PAT	30,000	37,500	37,500	34,500
-pref.- Dividend	-	7,500	-	
Profit for Equity shareholders	30,000	37,500	30,000	34.500
No. of equity shareholders	10,000	22,500	15,000	15,000
EPS	3.00	1.66	2.00	2.3

The above analysis reveals that the eps will be changed according to the composition of capital mix.

Illustration No. 3

Harish Engineering Company Limited provides the following financial information.

The company has 20,000 equity shares of Rs. 100 each. The company is in need of Rs.15, 00,000 to finance a major programme for expansion of business. The company product is well recognized by the customers in the market. It is searching for better alternative sources of finance, which will benefit the welfare of the shareholders. The following three alternatives are before company management. You are required to suggest best alternative method of raising financial resources.

(a) To issue of 15,000 equity shares of Rs.100 each
(b) To issue of 15,000 6% debentures of Rs. 100 each
(c) To issue of 15,000 8% preference shares of 100 each

The company is presently earning Rs. 10.00 lakhs (EBIT) the corporate tax is 50 per cent.

Solution:

Calculation of Earning Per Share at Different Levels of Capital Structure in Different Situations (Rs. in Lakhs)

Particulars	*Plan 1 (Equity)*	*Plan 2 (Debt)*	*Plan 3 (Preference)*
EBIT	10.00	10.00	10.00
-Interest	-	0.90	-
Profit after interest and before tax	10.00	9.10	10.00
50% income tax	5.00	4.55	5.00
Earnings after tax	5.00	4.55	5.00
-pref. dividend	-	-	1.20
Earnings available to equity share-holders	5.00	4.55	3.80
Number of equity Shares	35,000	20,000	20,000
Earning per share	14.28	22.75	19

The above analysis reveals that earning per share is highest when the company raises financial resources through issue of debentures.

Illustration No. 4

Vani Industries Ltd. present the following financial information.

The company has equity share capital of Rs. 10, 00,000. The face value of the equity share is Rs. 100 each. The company proposes to raise additional financial resources of Rs. 6,00,000 for expansion purpose of the business. It examines the following various alternatives in order to provide maximum return to the shareholders:

(a) By issue of equity shares.
(b) Rupees two lakhs in equity and four lakhs in debentures at 8 per cent.
(c) By issue of debentures at 8 per cent per annum.
(d) By issue of equity of Rupees two lakhs and Rupees four lakhs in preference share capital carrying with the rate of dividend at 10 per cent.

Presently the company is earning before interest and tax are Rupees 3, 00,000. The corporate tax is 50 per cent. Calculate the earning per share in all situations and suggest the best alternative method.

Statement Showing Calculation of Earning Per Share in Different Situations

Particulars	Situation I E only	Situation II E+D	Situation III D only	Situation IV E+P
EBIT	3, 00,000	3, 00,000	3, 00,000	3, 00,000
- Interest	-	32,000	48,000	-
	3, 00,000	2, 68,000	2, 52,000	3, 00,000
-tax 50%	1, 50,000	1, 34,000	1, 26,000	1, 50,000
PAT	1, 50,000	1, 34,000	1, 26,000	1, 50,000
-Preference Dividend	-	-	-	40,000
Profits Available for equity shareholders	1, 50,000	1, 34,000	1, 26,000	1, 10,000
No. of Equity				

Shares	16,000	12,000	10,000	10,000
Earning per share	9 30	11.1	12.60	11

From the above analysis, the company should select situation iii because issues of debentures are more beneficial to the company. The eps is more in case of debenture issues.

Illustration No. 5

M/s. Disturbs and Sons are searching for a project. The following financial information reveals about the project details.

A company requires a capital investment of Rs. 75, 00,000. Interest on loan is 8 per cent and corporate tax is 50 per cent. Calculate the point of difference for the project by taking into consideration of debt equity mix ratio is 2:1. As a financial consultant, suggest your opinion by keeping in view of the welfare of shareholders.

Solution:

The debt equity ratio is two; one therefore the company has two alternative methods to meet the objectives of the firm.

(a) The company can raise its financial resources by issue of equity shares for the entire amount of Rs. 75, 00,000.

(b) As per the debt equity mix norms, the required amount should be Rupees fifty lakhs and Rupees twenty-five lakhs. Debt financing is fifty lakhs and equity financing is Rupees twenty-five lakhs.

The Point of Indifference can be Calculated as Follows

$$\frac{(X\text{-}I1)\ (I\text{-}T)\text{-}PD}{S1} = \frac{(X\text{-}I2)\ (I\text{-}T)\text{-}PD}{S2}$$

X = Point Indifference

11 = Interest under alternative 1

12 = Interest under alterative 2

T = Tax rate PD= preference dividend

S1 = Amount of equity under alternative 1

S2 = Amount of equity under alternative 2 $\frac{50 \times 10}{100} = 5$

T = 50% S1=75 S2=25 11 = 0 12 = 8%

Substituting the Values in the Formula

$$\frac{(X\text{-}0)\,(1\text{-}.5)\text{-}0}{75} = \frac{(x\text{-}\,5)\,(1\text{-}.5)\text{-}0}{25}$$

$$\frac{\text{Or}.5x}{75} = \frac{5x\text{-}2.5}{25}$$

Or

$$\begin{aligned} 25\,(.5x) &= 75\,(.5x\text{-}2.5) \\ 12.5x &= 37.5x\text{-}187.5 \\ 25x &= 187.5 \\ X &= 187.5/25 = 7.5 \end{aligned}$$

The above information reveals that at point of indifference are Rupees seven lakhs and fifty thousand.

Illustration No. 6

Niteesh Engineering Company Limited provides the following financial information.

The net income of the company is Rupees 1,60,000. The company has Rs. 4,00,000 10 per cent debentures. Its equity capitalization rate is 12 per cent. As a financial consultant, calculate the value of the firm and overall cost of capital as per the net income approach. Please ignore corporate tax. You are further also requested to calculate the overall cost of capital and capitalization rate of the company, if it raises another Rupees two lakhs through debentures.

Solution:

Calculation of the Value of the Firm

Particulars	Rs.
Net income	1, 60,000
- Interest on 10% debentures of Rs. 4, 00,000	40,000

Earnings available to equity shareholders	1, 20,000

Equity capitalization rate	12%

Market value of equity	$1,20,000 \times \frac{100}{12} = 10,00,000$
Market value of debentures	4, 00,000
Market value of the firm	14, 00,000

Calculation of Overall Capitalisation Rate

$$\frac{\text{Overall capitalization rate}}{\text{Value of the firm}} = \text{earnings}$$

$$= \frac{1,60,000}{14,00,000} = 0.1148 \text{ or } 11.48\%$$

Calculation of value of the firm if debentures are raised further 2,00,000 (Upto 6,00,000)

Net Income	1,60,000
- Interest on debentures of Rs.6, 00,000	60,000
	1,00,000
Equity capitalization rate	12%
Market value of equity	$1,00,000 \times \frac{100}{12} = 833,000$
Market value of debentures	6,00,000
Value of the firm	14,33,000

$$\text{Overall capitalization rate} = \frac{1,60,000}{14,33,000} \times 100 = 11.16\%$$

From the above analysis of information, it reveals that increasing of debt content in capital structure leads to increase in value of the firm and the overall cost of capital has been reduced.

Illustration No. 7

The following financial information is related to two identical organizations. You are required to calculate value of the firms as per net income approach method.

The firms X and Y exists in the market. The two firms have identical in all respects including risk factors except for debt equity mix. Company X has issued 9 per cent debentures for Rs. 30 lakhs and Company Y issued equity only. The two firms earns 25 per cent before interest and taxes on their total assets of Rs. 50 lakhs. The corporate rate tax is 50 per cent. The capitalization rate is 15 per cent for an all equity company.

Solution:

Computation of Total Value of the Firms as per Net Income Approach

Particulars	*Company X*	*Company Y*
Earning before interest and tax 25 per cent on Rs. 50 lakhs	12,50,000	12,50,000
- Interest on debentures	2,70,000	-
	------------	------------
	9,80,000	12,50,000
- Income tax 50%	4,90,000	6,25,000
	------------	------------
Earnings available to equity shareholders	4,90,.000	6,25,000
	------------	------------
Capitalization value 15%	32,66,600	41,62,500
+ Value of debt	30,00,000	-
	------------	------------
Total value of the firm	62,66,600	41,62,500

Illustration No. 8

DLF Universal Ltd. is thinking about different financial plans. The related financial information is given below:

(1) Total investment to be procured from the market Rs. 8,00,000.

(2) Proposal of financing schemes

Scheme: (i) 100 per cent equity only

(ii) 50 : 50 : equity and debt only

(iii) Half equity and half preference share capital

The cost of debt is 9 per cent, preference shareholders are entitled to get dividend at 10 per cent, and income tax rate is 50 per cent.

The equity share will be issued at a premium of Rs. 20 with a face value of Rs. 10. The company is expected to get earning before interest and tax is Rs. 2,00,000.

With the available information, you are required to calculate earning per share, financial break-even point. Further, you are required to calculate the EBIT in different schemes of the company.

Solution:

Computation of Earning Per Share at Different Schemes

Particulars	*Scheme A E only (80,000)*	*Scheme B E+D (40,000)*	*Scheme C E + P (40,000)*
Earning before Interest and Tax	2, 00,000	2, 00,000	2, 00,000
Debt 9%	-	36,000	-
PBT	2, 00,000	1, 64,000	2, 00,000
-Income tax 50%	1, 00,000	82,000	1, 00,000
PAT	1, 00,000	82,000	1, 00,000
- Preference Dividend	-	-	40,000
Earnings available for equity share-holders	1, 00,000	82,000	60,000
Number of equity shares	80,000	40,000	40,000
Earning per share	1.25	2.50	1.50

From the above analysis, it is observed that the company's earning per share is very high when it raised finance through debentures.

(b) Computation of financial break-even point for each scheme

Scheme (a): The scheme does not contain any debt, there are not any fixed financial charges, and therefore financial break-even point for this scheme is zero.

Scheme (b): The scheme contains debt to the extent of Rs.4,00,000, and having fixed charges of Rs. 90,000 therefore the financial break-even point plan for the scheme is Rs. 90,000.

Scheme (c): The scheme contains preference shares and the firm's liability to pay dividend to the extent of Rs. 40,000. Hence, the firm has financial break-even point for this scheme is Rs. 40,000.

(iii) Computation of EBIT for different schemes among the plans for point of indifference between schemes A and B, schemes A, and C, schemes B and C.

The computation of point of indifference between A and B schemes

$$\frac{(x\text{-}Ii)\,(I\text{-}T)\text{-}PD}{S1} = \frac{(x\text{-}I2)\,(I\text{-}T)\text{-}PD}{S2}$$

$$\frac{(X\text{-}0)\,(1\text{-}0.5)\text{-}0}{80{,}000} = \frac{(x\text{-}36{,}000)\,(1\text{-}.5)\text{-}0}{40{,}000}$$

Or

$$\frac{.5x}{80{,}000} \qquad \frac{.5x\text{-}18{,}000}{40{,}000}$$

Or

$$40{,}000\,(.5x) = 80{,}000\,(.5\,x\text{-}18{,}000)$$
$$.5x = 8\,(.5x\text{-}18{,}000)$$
$$.5x = 4x\text{-}1,44{,}000$$
$$.5x + 4x = 1,44{,}000$$
$$4.5x = 1,44{,}000$$
$$X = 1,44{,}000/4.5{=}32{,}000$$

Hence, the range of earning in the scheme a and b is Rs. 32,000

The Point of Indifference Between Schemes A and C

$$\frac{(X-0)(1-0.5)-0}{80{,}000} = \frac{(x-0)(1-.5)-40{,}000}{40{,}000}$$

$$\frac{0.5x}{80,000} = \frac{0.5x - 40,000}{40,000}$$

$$\begin{aligned} 0.5x\,(40,000) &= 80,000\,(0.5x-40,000) \\ .5x &= 8\,(.5x-40,000) \\ .5x &= 4x-3,20,000 \\ 4.5x &= 3,20,000 \\ X &= 3,20,000/4.5 = 71,111 \end{aligned}$$

The Point of Indifference Between Schemes B and C

$$\frac{(x - 36,000)(1 - 0.5) - 0}{40,000} = \frac{(x - 0)(1 - 0.5) - 40,000}{40,000}$$

Or

$$\begin{aligned} .5x18,000 &= .5x-40,000 \\ .5x+.5x &= 40,000-18,000 \\ X &= 22,000 \end{aligned}$$

Illustration No. 9

Kasturi Industries provide the following information. You are required to calculate necessary parameters in order to satisfy the shareholders.

(a) Earning before interest and tax is Rs. 5,60,000
(b) Interest on debt 12 per cent 8,00,000
(c) Corporate tax is 50 per cent
(d) Equity share capital Rs. 10 face value, no. of equity shares 60,000
(e) Eps of the firm Rs. 8
(f) Market price of the share Rs. 80
(g) PE ratio of the company 05
(h) It has retained earnings 14,00,000
(i) The present requirement of the funds is Rs. 8,00,000
(j) The investment will earn the same rate as funds already invested
(k) It is informed that a debt equity ratio higher than 16 per cent will push the P/E ratio down to 4 per cent and raises interest rate on additional borrowings to 10 per cent. You are required to calculate the earning per share.

Solution:

Computation of Earning Per Share When it Raises Financial Resources through Different Schemes

Particulars	Scheme I Resources raised by debt (Rs. 8,00,000)	Scheme II, if Resources raised by equity shares (8,00,000)
Earnings before Interest and tax* (20% on EBIT)	5,60,000	5,60,000
-Interest on Debentures (old)	96,000	96,000
	4,64,000	4,64, 000
-Interest on New debt	80,000	–
P.B.T.	3, 84,000	4, 64,000
-tax 50%	1, 92,000	2, 32,000
Earnings available for equity share-holders	1, 92,000	2, 32,000
Number of equity shares	60,000	70,000
Earning per share	3.2	3.314

1. *Calculation of present rate of earnings

Capital employed at present

Equity share capital	6, 00,000
10% debentures	8, 00,000
Reserves	14, 00,000
	28, 00,000

Earnings before interest and tax given in the problem. 5, 60,000

Present rate of present earning before interest and taxes

$$\frac{5,60,000}{28,00,000} \times 100 = 20\%$$

2. According to second scheme, the no. of equity shares to be issued by the firm $\frac{8,00,000}{80} = 10,000$

After the issue of fresh equity, the total number of shares in the capital structure of the firm 60,000 + 10,000=70,000

The debt equity ratio if Rs. 8,00,000 is raised as debt.

$$\frac{16,00,000}{36,00,000} X 100 = 44.44\%$$

Illustration No. 10

XYZ Ltd. provides the following information. You are required to calculate the value of the firm as per net income approach.

The company is expected to earn annual earning before the payment of interest and tax of Rs. 3, 00,000. The company has Rs.12.00 lakhs with 8 per cent debentures. The cost of capital is 10 per cent.

Solution:

Statement Showing the Value of Firm and Overall Cost of Capital

Earning before interest and tax	3, 00,000
-Interest on debentures (8%)	96,000

Earnings available to equity shareholders	2.04,000
Capitalization rate Ke	10 per cent
Market value of equity S=NI/Ke	

$$S = \frac{2,04,000}{10} X 100 = 20,40,000$$

Market value of debt	12,00,000

Total value of the firm	32,40,000

Overall cost of capital = $\frac{\text{EBIT}}{\text{Value of the firm}}$

$$\frac{3,00,000}{32,40,000} \times 100 = 9.25\%$$

Illustration No. 11

ABC Ltd. is providing financial information related to its business operations. It is expecting annual EBIT of Rs. 1, 50,000

The company has Rs. 6,00,000 in 8 per cent debentures. The equity capitalization rate is 10 per cent. The company desires to redeem debentures of Rs. 2,00,000 by issuing additional equity shares for the same amount. You are required to calculate the value of the firm and the overall cost of capital

Solution:

Statement Showing the Value of the Firm

Particulars	*Rs.*
Earning before interest and tax	1, 50,000
-Interest on debentures	32,000

Earnings available to equity shareholders	1, 18,000

Equity capitalization rate ke	10 per cent
Market value of EQUITY (S) $\frac{118000}{10} X 100 =$	11,80,000
Market Value of the Firm	4,00,000

Total Value of the Firm	15,80,000

Overall cost of capital ke $\frac{1,50,000}{15,80,000} X 100 = 9.49\%$	

Illustration No. 13

Rajani Industries Limited provides the following information for your financial analysis.

The company has an EBIT of Rs. 2,00,000. The cost of debt is 9 per cent and the outstanding debt is Rs. 8,00,000. The overall cost of capital is 10 per cent. Calculate the total value of the firm as per net operating income approach.

Solution:

Statement Showing the Value of the Rajani Industries Limited

Particulars		*Rs.*
Earning before interest and tax		2, 00,000
Overall capitalization rate (k)		10 per cent
Market value of the firm (v)		
$\frac{2,00,000}{10} = 100$		20,00,000
Total value of debt		8, 00,000
		12, 00,000
Market value of equity S = V-B		
Equity capitalization rate ke	$= \frac{EBIT - I}{V - B} X 100$	
	$\frac{2,00,000 - 72,000}{20,00,000 - 8,00,000} X 100$	
	$= \frac{1,28,000}{12,00,000} X 100 = 10.66\%$	

Illustration No. 14

Supriya Industries Limited present the following information related to its capital structure. It expects a net operating income is Rs. 2, 00,000. It has Rs. 10, 00,000 debentures with 9 per cent interest rate. Calculate the value of the firm and equity capitalization rate as per the net operating income approach. The overall cost of capital is 10 per cent.

You are also required to measure the effect on value of the firm and cost of equity, if the debt is increased to Rs. 15,00,000.

Solution:

To calculate the value of the firm, it is necessary to find out the market value of the firm.

$$\text{Market value of the firm} = V = \frac{\text{Net Operating Income}}{\text{Overall Cost of Capital}}$$

$$V = \frac{2,00,000}{10} \times 100 = 20,00,000$$

Market value of the firm	=	20,00,000
-Market value of debentures	=	10,00,000

Total market value of equity		10, 00,000

Equity capitalization rate or cost of equity ke

$$= \frac{\text{Earnings available to equity shareholders}}{\text{Total market value of equity shares}}$$

$$\frac{2,00,000\text{-}90.000}{10,00,000}$$

$$= \frac{1,10,000}{10,00,000} \times 100 = 11\%$$

If the company debt is increased to Rs. 15 lakhs, the equity capitalization rate will be calculated as follows

$$Ke = \frac{EBIT - I}{V - B}$$

$$Ke = \frac{2,00,000 - 1,35,000}{20,00,000 - 15,00,000}$$

$$= \frac{65,000}{5,00,000} = 0.13 \text{ or say } 13\%$$

Illustration No. 15

Sumanth Industries Ltd. provides the financial information for financial analysis.

The company is expecting an earning before interest and tax of Rs. 8, 00,000. It has 10 per cent risk class. You are required to calculate the value of the firm and cost of equity as per net operating income approach. The company employs 9 per cent debt to the extent of 40 per cent, 70 per cent, or 90 per cent of the total financial requirement of Rs. 40 lakhs.

Solution:

Statement Showing Value of Firm and Cost of Equity Capital

Particulars	*40% debt*	*70% debt*	*90% debt*
EBIT	8,00,000	8,00,000	8,00,000
Overall cost Of capital	10%	10%	10%
Value of Firm (V) V=EBIT/ke	80,00,000	80,00,000	80,00,000
Value of 9% debt (D)	16,00,000	28,00,000	36,00,000
Value of Equity (V-d)	64,00,000	52,00,000	44.00.000
Net profit (EBIT–Interest)	6,56,000 (8.0-1.44)	7,48,000 (8.0-2.52)	4, 04,000 (8.0-3.96)
Cost of equity	10.25%	14.38%	9.18%

Ke will be computed as follows

$$Ke = \frac{\text{Net profit}}{\text{Value of equity}} \times 100$$

$$\text{Ke at 40\% debt } \frac{6,56,000}{64,00,000} \times 100 = 10.25\%$$

$$\text{Ke at 70\% debt } \frac{7,48,000}{52,00,000} \times 100 = 14.38\%$$

$$\text{Ke at 90\% debt } \frac{4,04,000}{44,00,000} \times 100 = 9.18\%$$

Illustration No. 16

Nitheesh Industries Limited and Dinesh Industries Ltd. are two identical organizations working in the same risk class. The two companies are same in every aspect except that Nitheesh Industries uses debt while Dinesh Industries does not. The levered firm has Rs.18,00,000 debentures with an interest rate of 9 per cent. The two firms earn 25 per cent before interest and taxes on their total assets of Rs. 30,00,000. Capital market is perfect and tax rate is 50 per cent. The capitalization rate is 12 per cent. Using net operating income approach, calculate the value of two firms.

Solution:

Computation Value of the Firm as per Net Operating Approach

Particulars	*Nitheesh Industries (Levered)*	*Dinesh Industries (Unlevelled)*
EBIT (25% on 30 lakhs)	7.50.000	7.50.000
-Interest	1, 62,000	–
	------------	------------
Taxable income	5, 88,000	7, 50,000
-Taxes	2, 94.000	3, 75,000
	------------	------------
Earnings available for Equity shareholders	2, 94,000	3, 75,000
	------------	------------
Equity capitalization Rate (Ke)	12%	12%

As per net operating income approach, the value of levered firm can be computed as follows:

Value of levered firm = VI= vu + BT

Vu = value of unlevered firm

BT = market value of debt

Therefore, the value of the unlevelled firm can be computed as follows:

$$Vu = \frac{\text{EBIT} \times (1-t)}{\text{Ke}} \qquad \frac{7,50,000 \times (1-.5)}{12} \times 100$$

$$= \frac{7,50,000 \times 0.5}{12} \times 100$$

$$= \frac{3,75,000}{12} \times 100$$

$$= 31,25,000$$

Therefore, the value of unlevelled firm can be calculated as follows:

= 31,25,000 + 18,00,000 (0.5)

= 31,25,000 + 9,00,000 = 40,25,000

The overall cost of capital can be computed as follows:
The cost of debt + cost of equity = overall cost of capital
The cost of debt should be calculated for Nitheesh Industries Ltd.

$$Kid = 9\% (1-0.5) = 4.5\%$$

$$Ke = \frac{\text{earnings available to equity shareholders}}{\text{Market value of equity}} = \frac{2,94,000}{40,25,000 - 18,00,000}$$

$$= \frac{2,94,000}{22,25,000} \times 100 = 13.2\%$$

$$K = 4.5\% \frac{(18,00,000)}{40,25,000} + 13.2\% \frac{(22.25.000)}{(40,25,000)}$$

$$K = 4.5\% (0.44\%) + 13.2\% (0.55\%)$$
$$K = 1.98\% + 7.425\% = 9.40\%$$

Overall Cost for Nitheesh Industries is 9.40 per cent.
Overall cost for Dinesh Industries is 12 per cent as given in problem.

Illustration No. 17

Sowmya Industries Limited is expecting an annual net operating income of Rs. 2, 00,000. The average cost of capital of the company is 9 per cent. The company has an initial debt of Rs. 10, 00,000 at 7 per cent rate of interest. Calculate the value of the firm as per net operating income approach.

Solution:

Computation of Valuation of Sowmya Industries Ltd.

Particulars	*Rs.*
Net operating income	2, 00,000
Market value of the firm	22, 22,222
2, 00, 000,/.09	
Market value of debentures	10, 00,000

Market value of equity s=v-d	12, 22,222

The cost of equity will be computed as follows:

$$Ke = \frac{\text{net operating income} - \text{interest}}{V - D}$$

$$= \frac{2,00,000 - 70,000}{12,22,222} = \frac{1,30,000}{12,22,222} = 10.6\%$$

Illustration No. 18

Aradhana Industries Limited is expecting an earning before interest and tax of Rs. 6,00,000. The firm has raised Rs. 40.00 lakhs by issue of equity with capitalization rate 14 per cent. Now the firm intends to redeem a part of capital by issuing debentures. The company has two options to raise debt to the extent of 30 per cent and 50 per cent of total funds. It is expected that for debt, financing upto 30 per cent the rate of interest will be 10 per cent and equity capitalization rate is expected to increase to 15 per cent. If the firm opts to 50 per cent debt then the interest rate will be 11 per cent and equity capitalization rate will be 18 per cent. You are required to compute value of firm and its overall cost of capital under different options.

Solution:

Particulars	*0% debt*	*30%debt*	*50%debt*
Total debt	-	12,00,000	20,00,000
Rate of interest	-	10%	11%
EBIT	6,00,000	6,00.000	6,00,000
-Interest	-	1,20,000	2,20.000
Profit after interest before tax	6,00,000	4,80,000	3,80,000
Capitalization rate Ke	14%	15%	18%
Value of equity	$\frac{6,00,000 \times 100}{14}$	$\frac{480000 \times 100}{15}$	$\frac{380000 \times 100}{18}$
	= 42,85,714	= 32,00,000	= 21,11,111

DIVIDEND THEORIES

Profit is the most important aspect for commercial enterprise. The real owners of the corporate sector are shareholders. The shareholders are entitled to enjoy the benefits of the business enterprise. The stakeholders are risk takers. Risk and return is the game of the business. Return is reward to the investors. Risk is a future chance of loss. The equity shareholders are adventurous investors. Profit is an important ingredient in the financial management of the corporate sector. The aim of the financial management is to maximize return to the shareholders.

Index